His 1858 Time Capsule

Edited by Ross E. Heller

by
Abraham Lincoln

His 1858 Time Capsule

Limited Forty-Four Copy
Editor-Signed
Presentation Edition
This is Number 29

Ross E. Heller

Published by

Seaside Books
Chevy Chase, Maryland

Habent sua fata libelli
Tiny books have their own destinies

by Abraham Lincoln: His 1858 Time Capsule
FIRST EDITION, FIRST PRINTING

Copyright © 2022 by Ross E. Heller
Publisher: CustomNEWS, Seaside Books
PO Box 15009
Chevy Chase, Maryland 20825
byabrahamlincolnbook.com

Library of Congress Cataloging In-Publication-Data has been applied for.
ISBN No.: 978-0-578-34029-6
Printed in the United States of America

Contents

Contents

Preface

In 1858 Abraham Lincoln casually and unknowingly created a time capsule of his contemporary mind-set on both slavery and race relations. Not hidden in a cornerstone, it took the form of a 3.25" x 5.78" black campaign notebook shared with Capt. James N. Brown a long-time friend and fellow campaigner.

43-years later a portion of the time capsule was published in 1901; publicized by three devotees of Lincoln and his legend: Ida M. Tarbell, J. McCan Davis and William H. Lambert.

Yet the full contents – sheltered, but not hidden – have had to wait until 2022 to be completely disclosed.

by Abraham Lincoln: His 1858 Time Capsule contains *every* word written in Lincoln's notebook as well as the fascinating story of its 164-year journey.

About This Book's Cover
A thoughtful, clean-shaven Abraham Lincoln is penning his 1858 letter to James N. Brown. The ominous, brooding, gray-blue background portrays looming antebellum storm clouds of which Lincoln was so surely aware.

A Note on Size
Lincoln's original notebook measured 3.25" x 5.78". All original pages are reproduced in a color closely matching that of the original.

Terms
'Scrap Book', 'Scrapbook' and 'campaign note book' are contemporary usages of 1858. For consistency, 'scrapbook' is this book's spelling. 'Time Capsule' is a 2022 summary. The running headline "by Abraham Lincoln" atop left-hand pages is a vector from his own handwriting.

Abraham Lincoln

Editor's Introduction

by Abraham Lincoln reproduces the *only* book actually hand-written by Lincoln. His words and 19th century news clips so crisply clear one can almost blot the ink, smell the aroma of his paste-pot. It is a time capsule into the 1858 mindset of the man who became the 16th President.

As well, it contains new facts pertaining to the telling of America's most-storied life; a life about which no one could imagine anything new could *ever* be found.

It was October 18 in the waning days of Lincoln's Senatorial campaign against Stephen A. Douglas when James N. Brown, a fellow campaigner and personal friend, beseeched him for a clear statement on the "paramount issue" of the day: "Negro equality". Lincoln acceded, annotating what he called a 'scrapbook' with news clips and a definitive 8-page letter.

The 'scrapbook' was cherished by Brown and, after his 1868 death, by his sons William and Benjamin. Eventually they sold it to New York rare-book dealer George D. Smith who found a customer in Philadelphia Lincoln collector William H. Lambert who believed Lincoln's words warranted wider distribution. Thus, a version of the notebook was published in 1901: *Abraham Lincoln His Book A Facsimile Reproduction of the Original with an Explanatory Note by J. McCan Davis.* After Lambert's death the 'scrapbook' was auctioned in 1914 and purchased for Henry E. Huntington's San Marino, California library.

Now, Lincoln's handwritten words vividly return. As well, there are contemporary notes from 1858 campaigner Brown. Distinguished Lincoln scholar Harold Holzer has provided a historical perspective; there is an extraordinary 'behind the scenes' peek how the 1901 *Facsimile* came to be; plus original artwork by renowned Lincoln portraitist Wendy Allen.

Ɛ Abraham Lincoln

Seen through a 21st century lens, Lincoln's statements are mile-markers on a road map. As David W. Blight said about Lincoln's "moral fiber" in his 2018 biography of Frederick Douglass: "Lincoln had always hated slavery and wished it somehow destroyed. . . . [and] he possessed a remarkable capacity to adapt, grow, and change on this most crucial question." Lincoln's words in this book confirm Blight's conclusion.

Special Introduction
The Words of Lincoln

By Harold Holzer

In distant Delhi, India, a prominent wall inside the Shri Ram School has long been adorned by a large poster featuring words from "Lincoln's Letter to his Son's High School Teacher":

He will have to learn, I know, / That all men are not just, / All men are not true, / But teach him also that / For every scoundrel there is a hero; / That for every selfish politician, / There is a dedicated leader.

Of course, Lincoln never wrote any such thing, to his son's teacher or anyone else, much less in free verse. Yet this so-called letter attained such power in India that it was eventually endorsed by its council of educational research and training, the body that runs that nation's primary and secondary school system.

Although the sentiments themselves are fake, they do, uncannily, remind us of a genuine challenge Lincoln faced throughout his career: the need to achieve success as a politician in order to earn the chance to demonstrate greatness as a leader. And Lincoln's *authentic* words have long been associated with both aspirations.

It might be noted that Lincoln mastered these skills—politics and leadership, not to mention great writing—without the benefit of training at institutions like the Shri Ram School. In 1858, the year he campaigned for the United States Senate, the former U. S. Representative was quizzed about his own formal schooling by the editors of a forthcoming Dictionary of Congress.

Tackling the potentially embarrassing question, Lincoln supplied a terse, one-word response to describe his education: "Defective." As a child in Kentucky, he sat in classrooms for only "short periods" of time, and later, in Indiana, attended school only "by littles." As he summarized these experiences: "There was absolutely nothing to excite ambition for education. Of course, when I came of age I did not know much."

What he did learn, he learned on his own, and directly from books. He memorized Shakespeare and the Bible, absorbed the

art of elocution, and mastered the law. And he practiced penman-
ship until he could write more legibly than many of his contempo-
raries (ask any grateful scholar forced to parse the indecipherable
scrawls of Horace Greeley or Salmon Chase). Always, Lincoln
labored to be well-understood—by great thinkers, high courts,
military chieftains, professional politicians, and common people
alike. How remarkable, then, that he morphed into a literary talent
of such repute that he earned the praise of writers like Leo Tolstoy,
Victor Hugo, Ralph Waldo Emerson, and Harriet Beecher Stowe.
As Stowe put it, Lincoln's words were "worthy to be inscribed in
letters of gold."

Here was an especially apt compliment, since gold is both rare
and precious. And while the prolific Lincoln would produce more
than a million words on such subjects as government, politics,
military operations, slavery, freedom, and the law, the self-effacing
writer composed vexingly little about his own life, and nothing
about the methods he employed to persuade others. To the frus-
tration of generations of historians, Lincoln never kept a diary (two
of his Cabinet ministers and one of his private secretaries did so),
never collaborated with his son on an autobiography (as did his
Secretary of State), and of course, never lived to write an autobiography. All we have from him of an introspective nature are two
sketches of his life, one brief and the other briefer, both written to
introduce himself to national audiences in the months leading up
to the 1860 Republican National Convention.

Widening this information gap, we have been left few clues
about Lincoln's creative process, beyond recollections that he
wrote slowly and kept notes and ideas on scraps of paper stuffed
inside the lining of his top hat. Worst of all, Lincoln saved few
preliminary notes to his speeches once they were composed and
delivered. He seemed so uninterested in his original manuscript
copies, even of masterpieces like his 1858 House Divided address,
that he never saw to their preservation. The only thing that con-
cerned him after their successful delivery was their accurate reproduction in the newspapers—so that those beyond his original
in-person audiences could read them. (Ironically, as historian Don

Fenrenbacher discovered decades later, House Divided appeared in the press with one of its key early paragraphs transposed with another.)

Astonishing as it is to comprehend, we have no original, autograph manuscripts of any of Lincoln's pre-presidential orations. What lines did he cross out, or add later? We do not know. Even in 1860, after carefully proofreading his Cooper Union Address so it could be faithfully printed by the *New York Tribune*, Lincoln made no effort save the sheets of paper on which he had composed the seven thousand words that helped make him president. Once he had seen to their accurate typesetting, he indifferently permitted the handwritten pages to be swept out of the *Tribune*'s composing room.

Not until Lincoln hired former Illinois newspaper editor John G. Nicolay as his personal secretary during the 1860 presidential campaign was an effort made at last to impose a filing system on the future chief executive. The subsequently preserved trove we now call the "Lincoln Papers" (now housed at the Library of Congress) did come to include assorted notes, drafts, and memoranda, but almost nothing from the pre-White House years. Historian Ronald C. White Jr. demonstrated both the scarcity and importance of such material by gathering and interpreting Lincoln's fragmentary sketches and scraps for his 2021 book: *Lincoln in Private. What His Most Personal Reflections Tell Us About Our Greatest President*. White's collection reveals a leader wrestling with the momentous issues of slavery, freedom, and equality, and, consistent with historical interpretation, evolving from a cautious but ambitious western politician into the nation-altering author of the Emancipation Proclamation. It is fair to say that Lincoln never expected that this fragmentary writing would ever reach a wide audience. His musings were preliminary and private, not meant to be preserved, much less shared for publication. Now another exception is at hand.

One more 19th-century writer who sensed Lincoln's unique approach to writing was a European-based, occasional columnist for the *New York Tribune* named Karl Marx. In 1863, Marx would compare Lincoln's style of argumentation to "the trite summonses that one lawyer sends to an opposing lawyer, the legal chicaneries and pettifogging stipulations of an *actionis juris*"—a court case. Marx meant the assessment as a compliment. "Others, when dealing with square feet of land, proclaim it 'a struggle for ideas,'" he admiringly observed. "Lincoln, even when he is dealing with ideas, proclaims their 'square feet.'" Here, Marx sensed, was profundity masked by understatement.

Marx might have been describing the very book you are holding in your hands—a small but illuminating collection of newspaper clippings, accompanied by handwritten annotations, which Lincoln originally created as a reference tool for the 1858 Lincoln-Douglas debates. Those famous three-hour marathons required the Senate candidates, Republican challenger Abraham Lincoln and Democratic incumbent Stephen A. Douglas, to speak at exhausting length extemporaneously—and spontaneity was never Lincoln's forte. So, he occasionally drew specially prepared notebooks of press clippings from his pockets, and used them to quote his carefully composed previous oratory precisely as it had been printed in the press. This is one of those surviving notebooks. And it is particularly important because Lincoln made use of it even after the debates had concluded.

The last of the seven took place in Alton, Illinois, on October 15, but with seven weeks remaining in the Senate campaign, both aspirants took to the hustings individually to rally voters in swing districts. Always rancorous, the campaign now grew increasingly bitter, with the focus threatening to turn from the issue Lincoln had tried emphasizing—the evils of slavery expansion—to the incendiary one that Douglas had stressed—the supposed horrors of racial equality. At several of his post-Alton stops, Lincoln felt the pressure: hecklers repeatedly taunted him with accusations that he favored the then-radical concept of legal and social parity for African Americans, as Douglas had repeatedly charged during their joint appearances. At one post-debate stop, Democrats in the crowd tried baiting the Republican by displaying a black doll bearing a sign, "Hurrah for Lincoln!"

The Republican candidate could handle rowdy crowds. He grew alarmed only when fellow politicians from his own party began questioning him on race as well: did he really want Blacks to serve on juries or vote in statewide elections—rights we now take for granted—positions that would place Lincoln well outside the political mainstream and doom him to certain defeat in 1858?

When one crucial supporter from his own home territory began expressing such fears, Lincoln decided he must again clarify his position for the record—in the narrowest terms—or risk forfeiting the political coalition he had assembled to unseat Douglas. To stanch the bleeding, Lincoln repurposed one of his debate notebooks—the original of the volume you are reading now—and before leaving his Springfield home town for a campaign stop at Meredosia, sent it, with an explanation, to a Sangamon County, Illinois politician.

The fortunate beneficiary was James N. Brown of Island Grove, like Lincoln an ex-Whig and former state legislator, now running again for the Illinois Assembly. That Lincoln took so much trouble to set the record straight with Brown suggests not only that he took seriously the recent "accusations" of egalitarianism, but that he meant Brown to share the exculpatory evidence with other conservative-minded legislative candidates. This was crucial, for under voting laws that persisted into the 20th century, legislatures, not popular votes, would determine the next U. S. Senator from Illinois. In 1858, Lincoln needed his supporters to win seats in the upper and lower houses of the Illinois Legislature in order to elect him to the Senate when they convened in early 1859. Lincoln's name was not even on the 1858 ballot.

To arm Brown with written proof of his middle-of-the-road views, Lincoln shared the notebook containing clips of some of his previous, published speeches, adding handwritten, introductory notations along with a long explanatory letter dated October 18, 1858. As the speech excerpts demonstrate beyond doubt, Lincoln did not at the time believe that free Black Americans were entitled to equal status in society or under the law. And we must take "Honest Abe" at his word. Yet the extracts show that he remained a steadfast opponent of slavery, especially its extension beyond the borders where it then existed. Moreover, he believed that both natural law and America's founding documents guaranteed the equality of all men.

As Lincoln declared in the explanatory letter to Brown, penned into the notebook itself: "I do not perceive I can express myself, more plainly, than I have done in the foregoing extracts. In four of them I have expressly disclaimed all intention to bring about social and political equality between the white and black races, and in all the rest, I have done the same thing by clear implication." Equality under the law, he seemed to be insisting, should not be an issue in the 1858 campaign for Senate.

But equality under God was a different matter. "I believe the declaration that 'all men are created equal' is the great fundamental principle upon which our free institutions rest," Lincoln reiterated to Brown, adding one more time "that Negro slavery is violative of that principle."

Still, Lincoln admirers may be disappointed by the narrowness of this clarification, not to mention the defensive tone permeating some of the extracts. But those who have studied the mid-19th century will understand that anything more humane would not only have ended Lincoln's chances for the Senate in 1858, but doomed him to political obscurity for the rest of his career. Such was the political reality in a state that barred free Blacks from passing through its borders.

What you are holding in your hands is not only a faithful, but a remarkably vivid, reproduction of the very notebook Lincoln sent James Brown—that is, the version finally released to the public two score years after its creation, in 1901, with an introduction by J. McCan Davis, and published in New York by McClure, Phillips & Co.

Thanks to Ross E. Heller, father of the new edition, it comes to modern readers complete the clippings he wanted to cite at the debates to remind voters of the extent and limits of his humanitarian impulses.

One cannot read Lincoln's words without acknowledging how much the subject of race in America has shifted since Lincoln first assembled his legalistic denial that blacks and whites could (or should) be treated equally. Importantly, Lincoln's own views altered so dramatically over the next seven years that, in what turned out to be his final public speech in April 1865, he became the first American president ever to advocate for Black voting rights.

Yet it must be acknowledged that even in their own day, these handwritten notes and clippings from 1858 show Lincoln as less than daring on this subject. Here he seems defensive, somewhat calculating, willing to demonstrate an aversion to Black rights if it could empower him to destroy Black slavery. We must also take into account what Lincoln once called the power of "public sentiment." If Lincoln hoped to win a Senate seat, displace Douglas, and go to Washington to oppose the spread of slavery, he could ill afford to exile himself to political oblivion before Election Day. While an ocean divided opponents of slavery from those willing to see the institution made perpetual and national, a gulf still separated the advocates of freedom and equality. This merely explains, rather than defends, Lincoln's position. There can—and should—be no denying the fact that in 1858, Lincoln, along with the preponderant number of white people, believed in their own "superior position," as he put it.

As this notebook further reminds us, the Republican Senate candidate had already made his position clear on the hustings—most infamously (judging by modern standards), at the Lincoln-Douglas debate at Charleston on September 18. There was a "physical difference between the white and black races," he declared that day, "which I believe will for ever forbid the races living together on terms of social and physical equality." Blacks should never serve on juries, vote, or marry white people, he said that day, though he did take pains to add (provoking "Cheers and Laughter"): "I do not understand that because I do not want a Negro woman for a slave I must necessarily want her for a wife. My understanding is that I can just let her alone."

His explanations did not bring him victory. As we know, Lincoln lost the Senate seat after all; voters chose more than enough Democratic state legislators to re-elect Douglas. But Lincoln, depressed at first, was soon assuring supporters that "the fight must go on."

As he began modifying his positions as presidential candidate and president, Lincoln likely felt relieved that Brown, the notebook's new owner, kept it private. (In later years, Brown even pasted-in a few "scraps" of his own.) Yet history must be seen without blinders, and as this keepsake perhaps painfully reminds us, the Abraham Lincoln of 1858 was a long way from the Lincoln of 1863 who did so much to end slavery, recruit and arm men of color, and at last affirm their right to participate in the democratic process.

Perhaps this notebook does not show Lincoln at his most enlightened—but instead, at his most lawyerly, precise, and meticulous, perhaps more reflective of Karl Marx's view of Lincoln's writing skills than Harriet Beecher Stowe's. Here is a political realist determined to attract support from every disaffected voter, from progressive abolitionists to regressive racists. And all in the name of arresting the spread of slavery into the West and, as Lincoln often, if perhaps over-optimistically put it, placing it "on the course of ultimate extinction."

But do read some of the clippings Lincoln chose to include for his own use—especially the section of his 1854 Peoria address, in which he powerfully decried the "monstrous injustice of slavery itself," which "deprives our republican example of its just influence in the world—enables the enemies of free institutions, with plausibility, to taunt us as hypocrites—causes the real friends of freedom to doubt our sincerity." Re-examine his stirring plea to establish a "standard maxim for free society," from a speech at Springfield in 1857; or the peroration of his final debate rejoinder at Alton on the "eternal struggle" between liberty and "enslavement," between despotism and "the common right of humanity." Even within the constraints of mainstream politics, Lincoln could find ways to remain eloquent about freedom.

This is no ordinary souvenir because, like America itself, it is in a sense a work in progress. The notebook consecrates Lincoln's limited early views on racial equality, but in its blank pages also reminds us of his enormous capacity for subsequent moral and political growth.

In today's politics, flip-flopping is frowned upon and mocked. Here s evidence of what preceded a glorious transfiguration—the empty notebook leaves that Lincoln later symbolically filled in with his end-of-life accomplishments. Here might be a challenge to all of us to reflect on our own limitations, acknowledge our shortcomings, and leave room for growth that makes a difference. Here is an irresistible opportunity for modern readers to use these blank pages to record our *own* thoughts on the divisive issues *we* confront more than a century-and-a-half after Lincoln engaged Douglas on the subject of race in America.

As Lincoln put it just a few months after assembling this keep-sake: "Writing...is the great invention of the world...very great in enabling us to converse with the dead, the absent, and the unborn, at all distances of time and space."

As Lincoln would have hoped, this gorgeous reproduction of his writing speaks both to the past and the future, and hopefully re-minding all of us occupying our own small slice of history that the time for broadening the promise of democracy is always short.

Harold Holzer is the Jonathan F. Fanton Director of the Roosevelt House Public Policy Institute at Hunter College in New York City, a post he assumed in 2015 after 23 years as senior vice president of The Metropolitan Museum of Art. He also served for six years as chairman of the Abraham Lincoln Bicentennial Foundation and the previous 10 years as co-chair of the U.S. Lincoln Bicentennial Commission. He is the author, co-author or editor of 52 books on Lincoln and the Civil War era including Lincoln at Cooper Union. *His recent* Lincoln and the Power of the Press: The War for Public Opinion *won the distinguished Gilder-Lehrman Lincoln Prize.*

The *"La Jolla Lincoln"*

If this oil portrait could talk; the stories it would tell.

For years American artist Stephen Arnold Douglas Volk's **(1856-1935)**[1] 1928 painting hung in the La Jolla, California library of legendary *San Diego Union* publisher James S. Copley. Quietly gazing down, it absorbed the gossip, cigar smoke and brandy fumes of politicians of all stripes who called on the king-making newspaperman.

Volk's lifelong interest in Lincoln began as a boy of four when his father, sculptor Leonard Wells Volk, cast a plaster face mask[2] of Lincoln in 1860. Legend has young Volk sitting on Lincoln's lap as his father worked.

From the mask, according to Harold Holzer's *Lincoln President Elect*, Volk produced "cabinet-size portrait sculptures", one of which "graced" Lincoln's own "family parlor." An image of the bust is found in Appendix G.

Professionally known as Douglas Volk, the artist used his father's busts as models, and his images have become iconic. One, painted in 1908, is in the National Gallery of Art collection. Another was used on the four-cent stamp from 1954-1968. And President Richard M. Nixon hung the 1931 "Lincoln, the Ever-Sympathetic" – now in the White House Lincoln bedroom – in his fireplace roaring, air-conditioned White House library.

[1] Volk was named for his mother's maternal cousin, Lincoln's 1858 Senatorial and 1860 Presidential rival.

[2] In *Lincoln President Elect* Holzer comments on mask making; quoting Lincoln telling another sculptor, Thomas D. Jones, in late 1860 the "process . . . was anything but agreeable" comparing it to "be[ing] assassinated through the custom of . . . tak[ing] a [plaster] cast of the face."

Nineteenth Century

by

Abraham Lincoln

His 1858 Time Capsule

On the following pages are Abraham Lincoln's hand-written notes to James N. Brown, transcriptions of the same and related news clippings pasted in by Lincoln.

Atop each note and clip is a "mssHN" key to that note's location in the original 'scrapbook' housed at the Huntington Library.

The transcription's spelling and punctuation (or the lack there-of) follows as closely as can be determined that which Lincoln used.

The following extracts are taken from various speeches of mine delivered at various times and places; and I believe they contain the substance of all I have ever said about ``negro equality'' The first three are from my answer to Judge Douglas, Oct. 16, 1854_ at Peoria_

mssHM 2144_p2

This is the *repeal* of the Missouri Compromise. The foregoing history may not be precisely accurate in every particular; but I am sure it is sufficiently so, for all the uses I shall attempt to make of it, and in it, we have before us, the chief materially enabling us to correctly judge whether the repeal of the Missouri Compromise is right or wrong.

I think, and shall try to show, that it is wrong; wrong in its direct effect, letting slavery into Kankas and Nebraska—and wrong in its prospective principle, allowing it to spread to every other part of the wide world, where men can be found inclined to take it.

This *declared* indifference, but as I must think, covert *real* zeal for the spread of slavery, I can not but hate. I hate it because of the monstrous injustice of slavery itself. I hate it because it deprives our republican example of its just influence in the world—enables the enemies of free institutions, with plausibility, to taunt us as hypocrites—causes the real friends of freedom to doubt our sincerity, and especially because it forces so many really good men amongst ourselves into an open war with the very fundamental principles of civil liberty—criticising the Declaration of Independence, and insisting that there is no right principle of action but *self-interest*.

Before proceeding, let me say I think I have no prejudice against the Southern people. They are just what we would be in their situation. If slavery did not now exist amongst them, they would not introduce it. If it did now exist amongst us, we should not instantly give it up.— This I believe of the masses north and south.— Doubtless there are individuals on both sides, who would not hold slaves under any circumstances; and others who would gladly introduce slavery anew, if it were out of existence. We know that some southern men do free their slaves, go north, and become tip-top abolitionists; while some northern ones go south, and be-

When southern people tell us they are no more responsible for the origin of slavery, than we ; I acknowledge the fact. When it is said that the institution exists, and that it is very difficult to get rid of it, in any satisfactory way, I can understand and appreciate the saying. I surely will not blame them for not doing what I should not know how to do myself. If all earthly power were given me, I should not know what to do, as to the existing institution. My first impulse would be to free all the slaves, and send them to Liberia,—to their own native land. But a moment's reflection would convince me, that whatever of high hope, (as I think there is) there may be in this, in the long run, its sudden execution is impossible. If they were all landed there in a day, they would all perish in the next ten days ; and there are not surplus shipping and surplus money enough in the world to carry them there in many times ten days. What then? Free them all, and keep them among us as underlings? Is it quite certain that this betters their condition? I think I would not hold one in slavery, at any rate ; yet the point is not clear enough to me to denounce people upon. What next?— Free them, and make them politically, and socially, our equals? My own feelings will not admit of this; and if mine would, we well know that those of the great mass of white people will not. Whether this feeling accords with justice and sound judgment, is not the sole question, if indeed, it is any part of it. A universal feeling, whether well or ill-founded, can not be safely disregarded. We can not, then, make them equals. It does seem to me that systems of gradual emancipation might be adopted ; but for their tardiness in this, I will not undertake to judge our brethren of the south.

When they remind us of their constitutional rights, I acknowledge them, not grudgingly, but fully, and fairly ; and I would give them any legislation for the reclaiming of their fugitives, which should not, in its stringency, be more likely to carry a free man into slavery, than our ordinary criminal laws are to hang an innocent one.

But all this; to my judgment, furnishes no more excuse for permitting slavery to go into our own free territory, than it would for reviving the African slave trade by law. The law which forbids the bringing of slaves *from* Africa; and that which has so long forbid the taking them *to* Nebraska, can hardly be distinguished on any moral principle ; and the repeal of the former could find quite as plausible excuses as that of the latter.

2

Judge Douglas frequently, with bitter irony and sarcasm, paraphrases our argument by saying "The white people of Nebraska are good enough to govern themselves, *but they are not good enough to govern a few miserable negroes!!*"

Well I doubt not that the people of Nebraska are, and will continue to be as good as the average of people elsewhere. I do not say the contrary. What I do say is, that no man is good enough to govern another man, *without that other's consent.* I say this is the leading principle—the sheet anchor of American republicanism. Our Declaration of Inddpendence says:

"We hold these truths to be self evident: that all men are created equal; that they are endowed by their Creator with certain inalienable rights; that among these are life, liberty and the pursuit of happiness. That to secure these rights, governments are instituted among men, DERIVING THEIR JUST POWERS FROM THE CONSENT OF THE GOVERNED."

I have quoted so much at this time merely to show that according to our ancient faith, the just power of governments are derived from the consent of the governed. Now the relation of masters and slaves is, PROTANTO, a total violation of this principle. The master not only governs the slave without his consent; but he governs him by a set of rules altogether different from those which he prescribes for himself. Allow ALL the governed an equal voice in the government, and that, and that only is self government.

Let it not be said I am contending for the establishment of political and social equality between the whites and blacks. I have already said the contrary. I am not now combating the argument of NECESSITY, arising from the fact

mssHM2_44_p6

2

that the blacks are already amongst us ; but I am combating what is set up as MORAL argument for allowing them to be taken where they have never yet been— arguing against the EXTENSION of a bad thing, which where it already exists we must of necessity, manage as we best can.

3.

In the course of his reply, Senator Douglas remarked, in substance, that he had always considered this government was made for the white people and not for the negroes. Why, in point of mere fact, I think so too. But in this remark of the Judge, there is a significance, which I think is the key to the great mistake (if there is any such mistake) which he has made in this Nebraska measure. It shows that the Judge has no very vivid impression that the negro is a human; and consequently has no idea that there can be any moral question in legislating about him. In his view, the question of whether a new country shall be slave or free, is a matter of as utter indifference, as it is whether his neighbor shall plant his farm with tobacco, or stock it with horned cattle. Now, whether this view is right or wrong, it is very certain that the great mass of mankind take a totally different view.— They consider slavery a great moral wrong; and their feelings against it, is not evanescent, but eternal. It lies at the very foundation of their sense of justice; and it cannot be trifled with.— It is a great and durable element of popular action, and, I think, no statesman can safely disregard it.

mssHM2144_p8

The fourth extract is
from a speech delivered
June 26 _ 1857, at Spring-
field_

The fourth extract is from a speech delivered June 26, 1857
at Springfield_

I think the authors of that notable instrument intended to include *all* men, but they did not intend to declare all men equal *in all respects.* — They did not mean to say all were equal in color, size, intellect, moral developments, or social capacity. They defined with tolerable distinctness, in what respects they did consider all men created equal—equal with "certain inalienable rights, among which are life, liberty, and the pursuit of happiness." This they said, and this meant. They did not mean to assert the obvious untruth, that all were then actually enjoying that equality, nor yet, that they were about to confer it immediately upon them.— In fact they had no power to confer such a boon. They meant simply to declare the *right*, so that the *enforcement* of it might follow as fast as circumstances should permit.

They meant to set up a standard maxim for free society, which should be familiar to all, and revered by all; constantly looked to, constantly labored for, and even though never perfectly attained, constantly approximated, and thereby constantly spreading and deepening its influence and augmenting the happiness and value of life to all people of all colors everywhere. The assertion that "all men are created equal" was of no practical use in effecting our separation from Great Britain; and it was placed in the Declaration, not for that, but for future use. Its authors meant it to be as, thank God, it is now proving itself, a stumbling block to all those who in after times might seek to turn a free people back into the hateful paths of despotism. They knew the proneness of prosperity to breed tyrants, and they meant when such should re-appear in this fair land and commence their vocation they should find left for them at least one hard nut to crack.

mssHM2144_p10

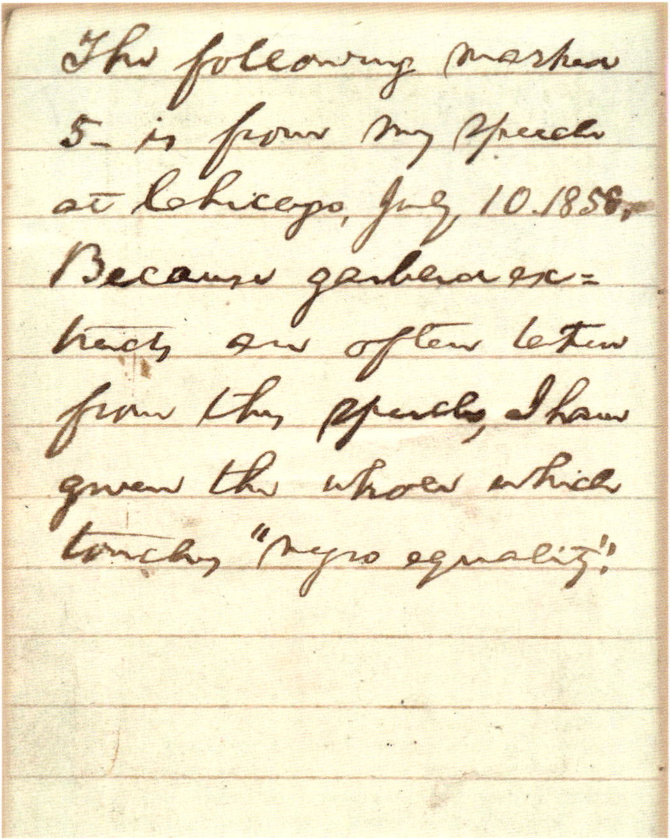

The following marked
5_ is from my speech
at Chicago, July 10. 1858.
Because garbled ex=
tracts are often taken
from this speech, I have
given the whole which
touches "negro equality".

The following marked 5_ is from my speech at Chicago, July 10. 1858. Because garbled extracts are often taken from this speech, I have given the whole which touches ``Negro equality.''

5

We were often—more than once, at least —in the course of Judge Douglas' speech last night, reminded that this government was made for white men—that he believed it was made for white men! Well, that is putting it in a shape in which no one wants to deny it, but the Judge then goes into his passion for drawing inferences that are not warranted. I protest, now and forever, against that counterfeit logic which presumes that because I do not want a negro woman for a slave, I do necessarily want her for a wife. [Laughter and cheers.] My understanding is that I need not have her for either, but as God made us separate, we can leave one another alone, and do one another much good thereby.—

There are white men enough to marry all the white women, and black men enough to marry all the black women, and in God's name let them be so married. The Judge regales us with the terrible enormities that take place by the mixture of races; that the inferior race bears the superior down. Why, Judge, if we will not let them get together in the Territories, they wont mix there. [Immense applause.]

A voice—"Three cheers for Lincoln."— [The cheers were given with a hearty good will.]

Mr Lincoln—I should say at least that is a self-evident truth.

Now, it happens that we meet together once every year, sometime about the 4th of July, for some reason or other. These 4th of July gatherings, I suppose, have their uses. If you will indulge me, I will state what I suppose to be some of them.

mss-M2144_p12

We are now a mighty nation, we are thirty—or about thirty millions of people, and we own and inhabit about a fifteenth part of the whole earth. We run our memory back over the pages of history for about eighty-two years and we discover that we were then a very small people in point of numbers, vastly inferior to what we are now, with a vastly less extent of country—with vastly less of every thing we deem desirable among men—we look upon the change as exceedingly advantageous to us and to our posterity, and we fix upon something that happened away back, as in some way or other being connected with this rise of prosperity. We find a race of men living at that day whom we claim as our fathers and grandfathers; they were iron men; they fought for the principle that they were contending for; and we understand that by what they then did it has followed that the degree of prosperity that we now enjoy has come to us. We hold this annual celebration to remind ourselves of all the good done in this process of time, of how it was done and who did it, and how we are historically connected with it; and we go from these meetings in better humor with ourselves; we feel more attached the one to the other, and more firmly bound to the country we inhabit. In every way we are better men in the age, and race, and country in which we live for these celebrations. But after we have done all this we have not yet reached the whole. There is something else connected with it.— We have besides these men—descended by blood from our ancestors—among us perhaps half our people who are not descendants at all of these men; they are men who have come from Europe—German, Irish, French and Scandinavians—men that have come from Europe themselves or whose ancestors have come hither and settled here, finding themselves our equals in all things. If they look back through this history to trace their connections with those days by blood, they find they have none, they cannot carry themselves back into that glorious epoch and make themselves feel that they are part of us, but when they look through that old Declaration of Independence they find that those old men say that "We hold these truths to be self-evident that all men are created equal," and then they feel that moral sentiment taught in that day evidences their relation to those men, that it is the father of all moral principle in them, and that they have a right to claim it as though they were blood of blood, and flesh of the flesh of the man who wrote that Declaration—[loud and long applause] and so they are. That is the electric cord in that Declaration links the hearts of patriotic and liberty-loving men together, that will link those patriotic hearts as long as the love of freedom exists in the minds of men throughout the world. [Applause.]

Now, sirs, for the purpose of squaring things with this idea of 'don't care if slavery is voted up or voted down," for sustaining the Dred Scott decision, [A voice—"Hit him again,"] for holding that the Declaration of Independence did not mean anything at all; we have Judge Douglas giving his exposition of what the Declaration of Independence means, and we have him saying it means simply that the people of America were equal to the people of England. According to his construction, you Germans are not connected with it. Now I ask you in all soberness, if all these things, if indulged in, if ratified, if confirmed and indorsed, if taught to our children and repeated to them, do not tend to rub out the sentiment of liberty in the country, and to transform this government into a government of some other form? What are these

14

5

arguments that are made, that the inferior race are to be treated with as much allowance as they are capable of enjoying; that as much is to be done for them as their condition will allow? They are the arguments that kings have made for enslaving the people in all ages of the world. You will find that all the arguments in favor of kingcraft were of this class; they always bestrode the necks of the people, not that they wanted to do it, but because the people were better off for being ridden. That is their argument and this argument of the Judge is the same old serpent that says you work and I eat, you toil and I will enjoy the fruits of it.

Turn it whatever way you will—whether it come from the mouth of a king, as excuse for enslaving the people of his country or from the mouth of men of one race as a reason for enslaving the men of another race, it is all the same old serpent, and I hold if that course of argumentation which is made for the purpose of convincing the public mind that we should not care about this, should be granted, it does not stop with the negro. I should like to know if taking this old Declaration of Independence, which declares that all men are equal upon principle and no making exception to it, where will it stop? If one man says it does not mean a negro, why may not another say it does not mean some other man? If that declaration is not truth let us get the statute book in which we find it and tear it out! Who is so bold as to do it? If it is not true let us bear it out! [Cries of " no, no,"] Let us stick to it then. [Cheers.] Let us stand firmly by it then. [Applause.]

It may be argued that there are certain conditions that make necessities and impose them upon us, and to the extent that a necessity is imposed upon a man he must submit to it.— I think that was the condition in which we found ourselves when we established the government. We had slaves among us, we could not get our constitution unless we permitted them to remain in slavery, we could not secure the good we did secure if we grasped for more, and having by necessity submitted to that much, it does not destroy the principle that is the charter of our liberties. Let that charter stand as our standard.

My friend has said to me that I am a poor hand to quote Scripture. I will try it again, however. It is said in one of the admonitions of the Lord, "As your Father in Heaven is perfect, be ye also perfect." The Saviour, I suppose, did not expect that any human creature could be perfect as the Father in Heaven; but He said, "As your Father in Heaven is perfect, be you perfect." He set that up as a standard, and he who did most towards reaching that standard, attained the highest degree of moral perfection. So I say in relation to the principle that all men are created equal. Let it be as nearly reached as we can. If we cannot give freedom to every creature, let us do nothing that will impose slavery upon any other creature. [Applause.] Let us then turn this government back into the channel in which the framers of the Constitution originally placed it. Let us stand firmly by each other. If we do not do so we are turning in the contrary direction, which our friend Judge Douglas proposes —not intentionally—as worknig in the traces tending to make this a universal slave nation. [A voice—"that is so."] He is one that runs in that direction, and as such I resist him.

mssHM2144_p16

My friends, I have detained you about as long as I desired to do, and I have only to say, let us discard all this quibbling about this man and the other man—this race and that race and the other race being inferior, and therefore they must be placed in an inferior position—discarding the standard we have left us. Let us discard all these things, and unite as one people throughout this land, until we shall once more stand up declaring that all men are created equal.

My friends, I could not without launching off upon some new topic, which would detain you so long, continue to-night. [Cries of "go on."] I thank you for this most extensive audience which you have furnished me to-night. I leave you, hoping that the lamp of liberty will burn in your bosoms until there shall no longer be a doubt that all men are created free and equal.

Mr. Lincoln retired amid a perfect torrent of applause and cheers.

mssHM2144_p17

The following marked 6, was brought in immediately, after reading the first extract in this scrap-book, in the first joint meeting with Judge Douglas, Aug_ 21_ 1858 at Ottawa_

mssHM2144_p18

Now gentlemen, I don't want to read at any greater length, but this is the true complexion of all I have ever said in regard to the institution of slavery and the black race. This is the whole of it, and anything that argues me into his idea of perfect social and political equality with the negro, is but a specious and fantastic arrangement of words, by which a man can prove a horse chestnut to be a chestnut horse. [Laughter.] I will say here, while upon this subject, that I have no purpose directly or indirectly to interfere with the institution of slavery in the States where it exists. I believe I have no lawful right to do so, and I have no inclination to do so. I have no purpose to introduce political and social equality between the white and the black races. There is a physical difference between the two, which in my judgment will probably forever forbid their living together upon the footing of perfect equality, and inasmuch as it becomes a necessity that there must be a difference. I, as well as Judge Douglas, am in favor of the race to which I belong, having the superior position. I have never said anything to the contrary, but I hold that notwithstanding all this, there is no reason in the world why the negro is not entitled to all the natural rights enumerated in the Declaration of Independence, the right to life, liberty and the pursuit of happiness. [Loud cheers.] I hold that he is as much entitled to these as the white man. I agree with Judge Douglas he is not my equal in many respects—certainly not in color, perhaps not in moral or intellectual endowment. But in the right to eat the bread, without leave of anybody else, which his own hand earns, *he is my equal and the equal of Judge Douglas, and the equal of every living man.* [Great applause.]

ⸯ Abraham Lincoln

The following, marked 7 is from my speech in the fourth joint
meeting, Sep, 18. 1858 at Charleston_

[*Lincoln on Negro Equality: His 1858 Campaign Notebook*
by historian Karl Yambert contains complete transcriptions of
Lincoln's newspaper clippings. Since the first sentence on the
opposite page is obscured, Yambert, who consulted additional
sources, offered this transcription: "While I was at the hotel
today an elderly gentleman called upon me to know whether I
was really in favor of producing a perfect equality between the
negroes and the white people [Great laughter.]"]

While I was at the hotel to-day a
gentleman called upon me to know whether I
was really in favor of producing a perfect
equality between the negroes and white people. [Great laughter.] While I had not proposed to myself on this occasion to say much
on that subject, yet as the question was asked
me I thought I would occupy perhaps five
minutes in saying something in regard to it.
I will say then that I am not, nor ever have
been in favor of bringing about in any way
the social and political equality of the white
and black races, [applause]—that I am not
nor ever have been in favor of making voters
or jurors of negroes, nor of qualifying them
to hold office, nor to intermarry with white
people ; and I will say in addition to this that
there is a physical difference between the
white and black races which I believe will for
ever forbid the two races living together on
terms of social and political equality. And
inasmuch as they cannot so live, while they
do remain together there must be the position of superior and inferior, and I as much as
any other man am in favor of having the
superior position assigned to the white race.
I say upon this occasion I do not perceive
that because the white man is to have the
superior position the negro should be denied
everything. I do not understand that
because I do not want a negro woman for a
slave I must necessarily want her for a wife.
[Cheers and laughter.] My understanding
is that I can just let her alone. I am now

in my fiftieth year, and I certainly never
have had a black woman for either a slave
or a wife. So it seems to me quite possible
for us to get along without making either
slaves or wives of negroes. I will add to this
that I have never seen to my knowledge a
man, woman or child who was in favor of
producing a perfect equality, social and political, between negroes and white men. I
recollect of but one distinguished instance
that I ever heard of so frequently as to be entirely satisfied of its correctness—and that is
the case of Judge Douglas' old friend Col.
Richard M. Johnson. [Laughter.] I will
also add to the remarks I have made, (for I
am not going to enter at large upon this subject,) that I have never had the least apprehension that I or my friends would marry negroes if there was no law to keep them from
it, [laughter] but as Judge Douglas and his
friends seem to be in great apprehension that
they might, if there were no law to keep them
from it, [roars of laughter] I give him the
most solemn pledge that I will to the very
last stand by the law of this State, which forbids the marrying of white people with negroes. [Continued laughter and applause.]
I will add one further word, which is this,
that I do not understand there is any place
where an alteration of the social and political
relations of the negro and the white man can
be made except in the State Legislature—
not in the Congress of the United States—and
as I do not really apprehend the approach of
any such thing myself, and as Judge Douglas
seems to be in constant horror that some such
danger is rapidly approaching, I propose as
the best means to prevent it that the Judge
be kept at home and placed in the State Legislature to fight the measure. [Uproarious
laughter and applause.] I do not propose
dwelling longer at this time on this subject.

Letter to James N. Brown

Abraham Lincoln's letter to James N. Brown, including a transcript, is found here and on the following pages.

mssHM2144_p22

Springfield, Oct. 18. 1858

Hon J. N. Brown

My dear Sir

I do not perceive how I can express myself, more plainly, than I have done in the foregoing extracts. In four of them I have expressly disclaimed all intention to bring about social and political equality between the white and black races, and, in all the rest,

I have done the same
thing by clear implica-
tion

I have made it equally
plain that I think
the negro is included
in the word "men" used
in the Declaration of In-
dependence —

I believe the declara-
that "all men are cre-
ated equal" is the
great fundamental
principle upon which

mssHM2144_p24

our free institutions rest;
that negro slavery is vi=
olative of that principle;
but that, by our frame
of government, that prin=
ciple has not been made
one of legal obligation;
that by our frame of gov=
ernment, the states which
have slavery are to re=
tain it, or surrender
it at their own pleas=
ure; and that all other
individuals, free states

and National government
— are constitutionally bound
to leave them alone about
it.

I believe our government
was thus framed because
of the necessity springing
from the actual
presence of slavery, when
it was framed.

That such necessity
does not exist in the
territories, where slavery
is not present—

In his (Mendenhall speech)
Mr Clay says
"Now, as an abstract principle, there is no doubt
of the truth of that de-
claration (all men created
equal) and it is desir-
able, in the original construction of society, and
in organized societies, to
keep it in view, as a
great fundamental prin-
ciple"

Again, in the same speech

Mr Clay says:

"If a state of nature
existed, and we were
about to lay the founda-
tions of society, no man
would be more strongly
opposed than I should
to incorporate the institution of slavery among
its elements;

Exactly so— In our
new free territory, a
state of nature does
exist— In them Con-

gress lays the founda-
tion of society; and,
in laying those founda-
tion, I say, with Mr
Clay, it is desirable
that the declaration
of the equality of all
men shall be kept
in view, as a great
fundamental principle;
and that Congress, which
lays the foundation of
society, should, like
Mr Clay, be strongly

opposed to the incorpo
ration of slavery among
its elements —
But it does not follow
that social and politic=
al equality, between whites and blacks,
must be
incorporated, because
slavery must not —
The declaration does
not so require —
Yours as ever
A. Lincoln

Transcript of the Lincoln Letter

Springfield, Oct. 18, 1858
Hon. J. N. Brown
    My dear Sir

I do not perceive how I can express myself, more plainly, than I have done in the foregoing extracts. In four of them I have expressly disclaimed all intention to bring about social and political equality between the white and black races, and, in all the rest, I have done the same thing by clear implication

I have made it equally plain that I think the negro is included in the word ``men'' used in the Declaration of Independence.

I believe the declaration that ``all men are created equal'' is the great fundamental principle upon which our free institutions rest; that negro slavery is violative of that principle; but that, by our frame of government, that principle has not been made one of legal obligation; that by our frame of government, the States which have slavery are to retain it, or surrender it at their own pleasure; and that all others---individuals, free-states and national government---are constitutionally bound to leave them alone about it_

I believe our government was thus framed because of the necessity springing from the actual presence of slavery, when it was framed.

That such necessity does not exist in the territories, where slavery is not present_

In his Mendenhall speech Mr. Clay says

``Now, as an abstract principle, there is no doubt of the truth of that declaration (all men created equal) and it is desirable, in the original construction of society, and in organized societies, to keep it in view, as a great fundamental principle''

Again, in the same speech Mr. Clay says:

"If a state of nature existed, and we were about to lay the foundations of society, no man would be more strongly opposed than I should to incorporate the institution of slavery among its elements;

Exactly so- In our new free territories, a state of nature does exist In them Congress lays the foundations of society; and, in

E Abraham Lincoln

laying those foundations, I say, with Mr. Clay, it is desirable that
the declaration of the equality of all men shall be kept in view, as
a great fundamental principle; and that Congress, which lays the
foundations of society, should, like Mr. Clay, be strongly opposed
to the incorporation of slavery among its elements_

But it does not follow that social and political equality between
whites and blacks, must be incorporated, because slavery must
not—

The declaration does not so require_

Yours as ever

A. Lincoln

James N. Brown

About James N. Brown

United Methodist Church, New Berlin, Illinois. This church was founded in 1822 and the building, which dates to 1862, is surrounded on three sides by the Woodwreath Cemetery on land donated by James N. Brown.

About James N. Brown

Absent James N. Brown, neither the 1901 *Facsimile* nor *by Abraham Lincoln* would exist.

Brown was a well-respected Sangamon County, Illinois, farmer, cattle breeder and occasional politician. For over 25 years his life intersected with his neighbor and personal friend, Abraham Lincoln.

Born in 1806, he was Lincoln's senior by three years, grew up in Kentucky and at one time was an owner of enslaved persons. As a young man, he served in the Kentucky militia obtaining the rank of Captain, a title he proudly kept the rest of his life. Later, moving to Berlin, Illinois, he emancipated his enslaved persons; many of them remaining in his employ for years afterward.

A part-time Whig politician, he served eight years in the Illinois House of Representatives including one term with Lincoln in 1840-1841. He was re-elected in 1842, 1846 and, after a break in service, in 1852.

In late 1857, discussing the politics of the day at what was later described as a "quiet conference of friends," Brown fatefully said: "My friends, I have been a Whig all my life. I cannot be a Democrat. From this time on, I am a Lincoln Republican."

According to a story, later described as of "trustworthy tradition," Lincoln arrived at the gathering just as Brown spoke. The words obviously impressed him. Thus, at a Republican meeting in early 1858 determining who was to run for the state legislature, Lincoln gently twisted Brown's arm: "You must run." Knowing his friend needed every legislative vote if he was to be elected Senator, Brown accepted Lincoln's entreaty, entering the campaign.

About James N. Brown

Jas. N. Brown [signature]

As the election drew near, Brown was assailed for his ties to Lincoln. Virulent opponents said Lincoln – and therefore Brown, by association – supported and wanted to bring about social and political "Negro equality."

Lincoln intervened. He went through his speeches, reproduced in newspapers of the day, of which he had previously pasted portions on the right-hand pages of his own personal small black campaign scrapbook. On seven of the blank facing pages he wrote explanatory notes to guide Brown as he campaigned. And, to nail home the point, added an eight-page letter to Brown.

Brown used the book during the campaign's waning days. It didn't help. He lost the election. But keeping it and, according to notes in the 1901 *Facsimile*, carrying "it with him in 1860 and in subsequent campaigns [as he] filled out the remaining leaves with many later newspaper scraps of his own selection". Not published in the *Facsimile*, Brown's handwritten and transcribed commentaries are, for the first time, reprinted on the following pages. The accompanying news clips are in Appendix B.

That Brown was a close friend of Lincoln's is further attested by Lincoln's giving him a signed first edition of the Follett, Foster and Company 1860 *Political Debates between Hon. Abraham Lincoln and Hon. Stephen A. Douglas*". According to the 2009 *Mr. Lincoln's Book: Publishing the Lincoln-Douglas Debates* by David H. Leroy, "only 42 volumes" of the approximately 30,000 – 50,000 copies printed "are known to be autographed by Lincoln."

Brown's copy of the *Political Debates* is in the Huntington Library. A scan of Lincoln's signature page is found in Appendix C.

In 1864 Baltimore as a Lincoln-supporting delegate, Brown attended the Republican – then known as the National Union party – convention. Not quite a year later, heartbroken, he was a pall bearer at Lincoln's May 4, 1865 Springfield, Illinois funeral.

When Brown died in 1868 his casket contained the mourning sash he wore on that somber 1865 day. His sons carried on his business interests and in 1911 he was honored by induction into the Illinois' Farmers' Hall of Fame. Discussing his role on the national stage, speaker Clinton L. Conklin said: "From a very early day [James Brown] was brought into intimate social and political association with Abraham Lincoln. They were both natives of [Kentucky.] They thought alike on the burning questions of the day about slavery."[1]

As he sought office in 1858, a campaigning James N. Brown utilized Lincoln's written and spoken words to echo his own views. In 2022, we recognize Lincoln's words as a glimpse into his evolving position on race relations, an issue bedeviling Americans to this day.

For this peek into Lincoln's state of mind; thank you, James N. Brown.

[1] Clinton L. Conklin's Illinois' Farmers' Hall of Fame comments are available at: https://hdl.handle.net/2027/uiug.30112049812388

About James N. Brown

Capt. James N. Brown is buried in Woodwreath Cemetery, New Berlin, Illinois. Photo by Charles T. Hitt, great-great grandson of James N. Brown.

James N. Brown's Notes and Transcripts

That the notes of James N. Brown are jumbled is an understatement. They may reflect whether Brown is responding to speakers he has just heard, news clippings, or other campaign materials. However, they are representative of typical arguments of the period, especially over expansion of slavery.

Brown wrote these notes at different times. Based on the context of the notes, those written in pen (pages 40-50) were likely from 1858. Notes in pencil (pages 52-66) were likely written around 1860.

The pasted-in news clips found in Appendix B were likely part of Brown's campaign resources; items helping him support his arguments. They are in the same order as in the 'scrapbook' with "mssHN" numbers referring to the Huntington Library's pagination.

Obviously misspelled words have been corrected. Items in brackets are unclear.

Transcripts follow Brown's written words.

all men are created
equal — that They are
endowed by their Creator
with certain inalienable
rights — that among these
are life liberty and the
persuit of happiness —
that to secure these ends
governments are instituted
among men, disiriving
their just powers from
the consent of the governed

mssHM2144_p31

All men are created equal __that they are endowed by their
Creator with certain inalienable rights__ that among these are
life liberty and the pursuit of happiness__ that to secure these
ends Governments are instituted among men, deriving their just
powers from the consent of the governed

& beseach you to keep
clear of Abolition party

M.ᵣ Bassett said that the
original Toombs bill did
not contemplate referring
the Constitution to the
people, and said that
it only requires 3 grains

mssHM2144_p35

[6 lines obscured by clipping]
& beseech you to Keep Clear of Abolition party. Mr. Bassett
says that the original Toombs bill did not contemplate referring
the Constitution to the people, and says that it only requires 3
grains

[While the transcription refers to "Bassett" it is possible Brown
wrote "Barrett" though it is presumed he knew how his opponent's name was spelled.]

[The 'Toombs bill' was introduced into the U.S. Senate by Georgia Sen. Robert A. Toombs who ultimately resigned his office
to join the Confederacy. According to Wikipedia this legislation
"proposed a constitutional convention in Kansas under conditions that were acknowledged by various anti-slavery leaders
as fair." However, the bill "did not provide for the submission of
the proposed state constitution to popular vote, where, ... it
[likely] would have been soundly defeated."]

now let us examine this
bill for a moment—
Mr Short has said and
May say to day that he
holds Cook & Brown as
the advocate of all that
he looks upon as bad
in his zeal for Douglass-
and therefore has a right
to charge them on them
in this canvass—
Wolves in sheep's clothing

mssHM2144_p36

[most of line obscured by clipping] Grains [?]
[most of line obscured by clipping] it___
now let us examine this bill for a moment – Mr. Short has said
and may say today that he holds Cook & Brown as the advocate
of all that he looks upon as bad in his zeal for Douglass—and
therefore has a right to charge them on them in this canvass –
wolves in sheep's clothing.

[Short was a legislative candidate running against Brown and
John Cook.]

do— to Call off attention
from us, in advocating
Whig principals —
at Mechanicksburg
I gave my definition
of that Claus of the
declaration which
Mr Short said that
I said a Negro in
africa was as good as
a Negro in africa—
Now I tell you what
I did say —

mssHM2144_p37

below words obscured by clipping
do_ to call off attention from us, in advocating Whig principles.
At Mechanichsburg I gave my definition of that Clause of the
Declaration which_ Mr. Short said that I said a Negro in Africa
was as good as a Negro in Africa__ Now I tell you what I did say

—

we Charge on the
democratic party
that they favour slavery —
now the evidence —
Mr Short said in his
hostility to the poor Af-
=rican, that no man
is his equal who puts
himself on an equality with
the negro — let us see
R. M. Johnson —

mssHM2144_p38

Below lines obscured by clipping
we charge on the democratic party that they favor slav-
ery_____ now for the evidence__ Mr. Short says in his hostility to the poor African, that no man is his equal who puts himself
on an equality with the Negro – let us see R. M. Johnson__

Mr. Webster is supposed to have
backward, he made these remarks:
"Sir, wherever there is a particular good
be done, wherever there is a foot of land
be staid from becoming slave territory, I a
ready to assert the principle of the exclus
of slavery. I am pledged to it from the ye
1837. I have been pledged to it again, a

Scott decision, and
showing how slaves
may be kept out
under that decision
said. Can not the
Territorial Legislature
and will it not be
Constitutional pass a
law that all men
shall recieve a fair
compensation for ther
labour —

mssH M2144_p39

near ines obscured by clipping
Dred Scott Decision, and showing how slavery may be kept out
under that decision says, Cannot the Territorial Legislature and
will it not be Constitutional pass a law that all men shall receive a
fair compensation for their labor __

mssHM2144_p41

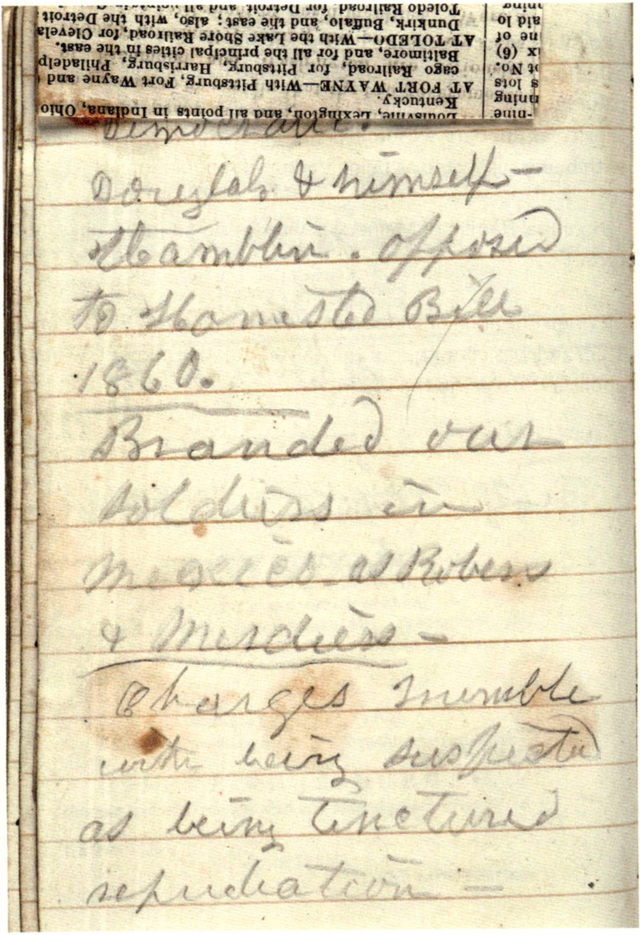

Louisville, Lexington, and all points in Indiana, Ohio
Kentucky.
AT FORT WAYNE—With Pittsburg, Fort Wayne and
cago Railroad, for Pittsburg, Harrisburg, Philadelp
Baltimore, and for all the principal cities in the east.
AT TOLEDO—With the Lake Shore Railroad, for Clevela
Dunkirk, Buffalo, and the east; also, with the Detroit
Toledo Railroad, for Detroit and all

Democrat.
Douglas & himself —
Hamblin. Opposed
to Homestead Bill
1860.
Branded our
soldiers in
Mexico as Robbers
& Murderers —
Charges Trumble
with being suspected
as being tinctured
repudiation —

mss HM2144_p41

Possibly one line covered by clipping
Democratic. Douglas & himself_____ [Hannibal]Hamlin. opposed to Homestead Bill 1860. _____ Branded our soldiers in
Mexico as Robbers & Murderers_____ Charges [Lyman] Trumbull
with being suspected as being tinctured repudiation__

[Hannibal Hamlin of Maine was Vice President in Lincoln's first
term.]

[Lyman Trumbull of Illinois was elected to the U.S. Senate in
1855 and was co-author of the Thirteenth Amendment, which
abolished slavery in the U.S.]

mssHM2144_p42

a lazy man
great ?Mckey..
Cables cavils ?Kents
Antago?nim
brought out Lincoln
beat him 58—

mssHM2144_p42

Possibly two lines under clipping
a lazy man Great [Mckey/Mehey/Mchey] Cables cavils
[Theretos] antagonisms brought out Lincoln ___ beat him 58—

Do the territories exercise
the rights of the state
can they do it —
who support it.
the stand which the
Tories took —
can draw no distinc
-tion — are you for the
boys and against the
fathers —
Histories of Parties —
What is it our business
to take any interest. Kansas
who paid the debts
for public domain

mssHM2144_p44

Do the Territories exercise the rights of the States can they do it__ who Support it they Stand where the Tories stood_____ can draw no distinction —are you for the _____Tories and against the Fathers_____ Histories of Parties _____ What is it our business to take any interest. Kansas _____ who paid the debts for Public domain.

mssHM2144_p45

Hatford Convention
Whig Party — Fedrator
— Past with Person
Mr Clay said _____
would ____ ___
Mr Clay take all
shabby sheep —
abolition party Republican
white trash cook her
King George said we
our squatters —.
600 Negros at the
Lincoln Meeting Using

mssHM2144_p45

Hartford Convention _____ Whig Party Federation __ Past
with [Sorsden] Mr. Clay said [Juptor/Sufton] would __Cus__ Mr.
Clay takes all shabby sheep__ Abolition party. Republican White
trash Cook here King George—Said we were squatters__ 600
Negros at the Lincoln Meeting Spring—

Extraordinary efforts.

Mans. Rights, advocated by
the democratic Party —

If I dont [now] that Democatic
stand when the Dem & whig
party stood in 1858 — he would bане
the stand —

Dem — No — new principal
everything says the prim 4 years.
(C)

Self government —
Popular Government —
I say I meant popular Gov.
was settled by Pilgrims —
Bristow says 76 —

mssHM2144_p46

Extraordinary efforts _____ Mans. rights advocated by the Democratic Party__
_____ If I don't prove that Democratic stand where the Dem & Whig party stood in 1850__he would leave the stand__ Dem No_ new principal Douglas says the prin 4 years old _____ Self government_____ Popular Sovereignty _____ I 58 I referred popular sovereignty was settle by Plgams__ Bristo says 76—

local Legistatures – colinies of
Great Britan –

[illegible] of the territories
King George & Parlement –

1850 Compromies settle the
attention slavery quistion
report of Clay –
to avoid in all future
time the agitation out of
congress –

he thinks I will not today
advocat. Mr Clay. tells us the
reasons why he wished congress to
refrain –

he did not tell us that
slavery existed by the law of [illegible]

mssHM2144_p47

local Legislatures . . colonies of Great Britain. _____ Ma unity of the territories King George & Parliament_____ 1850 Compromises settled this attention slavery question _____ report of Clay— To avoid in all future time the agitation out of Congress— he thinks I will not today advocate. Mr. Clay tells us the reasons why he wished Congress to refrain. _____ he did not tell us that slavery existed by the laws of Mexico.

Wilmot proviso —
who did Mr resist it —
Mr Clay — Mr Compromise
New sect — admit the
right of Congress — to legis=
Republican are not respons
=ible for what Editors & all
others may say = he was going
show that Clay —
He has garbled from
Mr Clay — senator from slave
state — read the connection
Have the republican
said that Slavery should
not go in to territory when

mssHM12144_p48

Wilmot proviso__ which did Mr. resist it. Mr. Clay__ Mo.
Compromise _____ New Section__ admit the Right of Congress __to Legis _____ Republican are not responsible for what
Editors & all others may say = he was going show that Clay— He
has garbled from Mr. Clay__ Senator from slave State. read the
connection Have the republican said that slavery should not go
in to Territory where [when?]

slavery existed.

~~Mr Clay~~ Plan as a

Senator. not as a man

Douglas says the people

free to do as they please—

He asks me if I would place

this power in congress.

mssHM2144_p49

Slavery existed__ Mr. Clay Plan as a Senator_ not as a man
Douglas says the people free to do as they please _____
He asks me if I would place this power in Congress____

Abraham Lincoln

J. McCan Davis

J. McCan Davis's "Explanatory Note"

On the following pages is the *Facsimile's* "Explanatory Note" by
J. McCan Davis (1866 – 1916). An Illinois journalist who wrote ex-
tensively on the life of Lincoln, in 1896 he assisted Ida M. Tarbell
in compiling her book *"The Early Life of Abraham Lincoln."* And in
1909 wrote his own: *"How Abraham Lincoln Became President.
Centennial edition 1809-1909."*

In the "Explanatory Note," Davis tells in detail how Lincoln's
"scrapbook" came to be written. And he acknowledges James N.
Brown's sons, William and Benjamin, "to whom we are indebted
for the facts pertaining to its history."

Davis's essay surveys the Illinois political scene of the late
1850's. Then he provides a brief biography of Brown as well as
how Lincoln gently twisted his arm to run for the Legislature in
1858. Critically, Davis's goes into depth about the 1858 Senatorial
campaign's issues.

"Popular feeling was intensified as the campaign progressed,"
Davis writes. "Entering upon his canvass Captain Brown was confronted everywhere with the charge that Lincoln stood for 'negro
equality,' social and political." According to Davis, "Personally, of
course, Captain Brown understood Lincoln's position perfectly"
but "felt the necessity for something authoritative – a statement
from Mr. Lincoln himself, setting forth his views in lucid and
unmistakable language."

The result: the little "small pocket memorandum book" containing "the most recent and authoritative statement of his views
which he could possibly have made." Davis's essay underscores
Brown's election defeat, saying "no argument was strong enough
to overcome the prejudice then so widespread and unreasoning."

ᔆ Abraham Lincoln

As to how Lincoln's handwritten words came to be published, he concludes with a single sentence: "In 1900 the book was sold by the Messrs. Brown to Mr. William H. Lambert of Philadelphia." Glossed over: the three-year back-and-forth details described in the following chapter.

Interestingly, Davis, himself, left a handwritten note for posterity. Kept in the Huntington Library's clamshell box with the notebook is a slender slip of a "bookmark" which states: "Lincoln's part of the book ends here. Pages which follow were prepared subsequently by Mr. Brown." It is signed: "J. McCan Davis," and is found in Appendix C.

LINCOLN: HIS BOOK

AN EXPLANATORY NOTE.

ABRAHAM LINCOLN—HIS BOOK.

This book—the only one now or ever extant of its illustrious authorship—owes its existence to the political campaign of 1858, when the opposing candidates for United States Senator from Illinois were Abraham Lincoln and Stephen A. Douglas. The issue was slavery—whether, as Mr. Lincoln contended, it should be restricted to the states in which it already existed, or, as Judge Douglas advocated, it should be permitted to invade the new territories if agreeable to the people thereof.

Mr. Lincoln, at that time, did not advocate emancipation. He made no demand for the liberation of the slaves then in bondage. He made no plea for negro citizenship. While he regarded slavery, as he had declared as early as 1837, as "founded on both injustice and

— 2 —

bad policy," and of course hoped for its "ultimate extinction," he recognized its constitutional status in the states in which it then had an existence, and, without any purpose to disturb it there, raised his voice only against its further extension.

His position, however, was constantly misstated by his opponents. Judge Douglas made the charge of "abolitionism," and the accusation was reiterated throughout the state, from the beginning to the end of the campaign, by Democratic orators and newspapers. It was charged that Lincoln stood for the equality of the races, politically and socially; and it was pointed out, with alarm and indignation, that should his doctrines prevail, there would be inevitable social and political chaos. Whites and blacks would intermarry promiscuously; the impassable line which had so long separated the two races would be wholly obliterated; the hated black man would be invested with political privileges which hitherto had been counted the white man's exclusive and sacred rights.

— 3 —

There were few sections of Illinois where prejudice against the negro was stronger than in Sangamon county, the home of Mr. Lincoln. The city of Springfield and the adjacent country was inhabited largely by natives of Kentucky. Before coming to Illinois they had been accustomed to slavery, and, while many agreed with Mr. Lincoln that the institution was fundamentally wrong and ought to be restricted, the remotest suggestion of making a negro their social and political equal was abhorrent. It was this prejudice that kept so many of the Whigs, even after their party was manifestly doomed to extinction, from joining the new Republican party. It was this influence that gave Fillmore his strength in Illinois in 1856, and, by dividing the anti-Democratic forces, gave the state's electoral vote to Buchanan.

The widespread fear of "negro equality" was at once recognized by Mr. Lincoln as the most portentous obstacle to the success of the new party. It made the Old Line Whigs —his life-long political associates– hesitant,

— 4 —

wavering, and distrustful. Some of them had already gone over to the Democracy.

In 1857 there was no longer any doubt that the Whig party could never survive another election. It was, in truth, already dead. Many of the Old Whigs of Sangamon county were still at sea, not knowing whither to turn for safe and congenial affiliations. There were really but two courses open—they must join the new Republican party, with its advanced and distrusted doctrines on slavery, or they must join the pro-slavery Democracy, which they had been fighting from time immemorial.

It was this dilemma which brought together, one day in that year, a few Sangamon county men who long had been prominent in the Whig party councils. The assemblage, in a retrospective view, was notable and historic, though at the time it was but a quiet conference of friends, for whose proceedings we are indebted wholly to a trustworthy tradition. There were present, among others, Judge Stephen T. Logan and Major John T. Stuart,

— 5 —

both of whom had been Lincoln's law part-
ners; Colonel John Williams, Major Elijah
Iles, and Captain James N. Brown. There was
a full and frank discussion of the difficult
problem. Every one present expressed his
views and intentions. Some had joined the
Republicans in the previous year; others
were now ready to do so, while several, like
Major Stuart, although not yet prepared to go
with the Democracy, declared that they never
could be Republicans.

Captain Brown, when called upon to state
his position, said: "My friends, I have been a
Whig all my life. I cannot be a Democrat.
From this time on, I am a Lincoln Republican."

Mr. Lincoln, up to this point, had not been
present; but he stepped into the room just in
time to hear Captain Brown's declaration.

This conference was followed by another
early in 1858. It was a Republican meeting
this time, and of great local importance.
Captain Brown was there, and so was Lincoln.
The matter under consideration was the per-

— 6 —

sonnel of the local ticket for the campaign
then about to open. The master spirit of the
occasion was Mr. Lincoln. He talked at length
and emphasized the importance of a policy
which would set at rest the minds of the Old
Whigs who still remained practically without
a party—showing them that the new party
was not the exponent of "abolitionism," as
had been alleged against it, but that it stood
only for the conservative doctrine of the restriction of slavery to existing limitations.
Captain Brown, like Lincoln, was a native of
Kentucky, coming of a distinguished family
of that state (his father, Colonel William
Brown, a veteran of the war of 1812, having
served in Congress with Henry Clay, defeat-
ing Colonel Richard M. Johnson, who was subsequently United States Senator and Vice-
President). He had been a life-long Whig,
and, like many of his party associates, had
kept out of the Republican party in 1856,
voting for Fillmore. He had long been a personal friend of Lincoln, and was, moreover, a
man of blameless reputation.

Mr. Lincoln, at this meeting, urged the nomination of Captain Brown as one of the party's candidates for the legislature. Brown did not want the nomination, and said so; he had served four terms in the House (including one term with Lincoln, back in 1840 and '41), and was now averse to longer public service. But Lincoln was insistent, and made an argument which disclosed in him the astute politician that all recognized him to be.

"You must run," he said to Brown. "We cannot, must not, nominate an Eastern man; he would be beaten. We must have the votes of the Old Line Whigs. You have been a Whig; you are a Kentuckian; you have been a slave-holder. You will get the support of the large conservative element—the Old Line Whigs and the men of Southern birth and sympathies who, while willing to let slavery remain where it is, are with us against its further extension, but who would be afraid to trust an Eastern man," and he called off the names of a half-hundred Old Line Whigs of local prominence who would

— 8 —

vote for such a man as Brown, but would oppose a candidate of Eastern birth or of doubt-
ful antecedents.

Captain Brown, persuaded to an acceptance by Lincoln's unanswerable logic, was
later nominated for the lower branch of
the General Assembly, his associate on the
ticket being John Cook, son of a Kentuckian,
and afterwards a Union General in the Civil
War.

Popular feeling was intensified as the campaign progressed. The old prejudice against
the negro, inbred in the men of Southern
nativity—the heritage of many generations
of perverted opinion—was found deep-rooted
and bitter. Entering upon his canvass, Captain
Brown was confronted everywhere with the
charge that Lincoln stood for "negro equality," social and political.

"Why, Brown!" his old friends would say,
in astonishment, "How can you, a Kentuckian, yourself once a slaveholder, stand
for a Black Abolitionist—a man who says the
negro is your equal and mine?"

— 9 —

Personally, of course, Captain Brown understood Lincoln's position perfectly; but there were many whom he found it impossible to convince that Lincoln held no such views as were ascribed to him.

He felt the necessity for something authoritative—a statement from Mr. Lincoln himself, setting forth his views in lucid and unmistakable language. Late in the campaign he asked Mr. Lincoln for such a statement. Mr. Lincoln went over his published speeches for several previous years, including those in his debate with Douglas just then concluded, and clipped out whatever he had said on the subject of "negro equality." These extracts he pasted into a small pocket memorandum book, making explanatory notes wherever needed. He supplemented this printed matter with a letter addressed to Captain Brown, filling eight pages of the little book. This letter, containing the essence of all he had previously said, was the most recent and authoritative statement of his views which he could possibly have made, and it was precisely the

— 10 —

thing which his friend and supporter had felt the need of throughout his canvass.

The close of the campaign was near, only about two weeks of it remaining, but the time was fully utilized by Captain Brown. He carried the book in his pocket, and whenever Lincoln's "negro equality" views were questioned—and this must have been many times every day, in the course of his public speeches and private conversations—he would produce the book and read from it " Lincoln's own words," placed there by Lincoln himself only a few days before.

But no argument was strong enough to overcome the prejudice then so widespread and unreasoning, and both legislative candidates (one of Southern birth, and the other of Southern ancestry) failed of election.

The book, of course, had been intended by Mr. Lincoln only to meet a temporary requirement, and very likely he had no idea that it would survive the campaign of 1858; but Captain Brown carefully preserved it and must have carried it with him in 1869 and in subsequent campaigns, for he filled out the remaining leaves with many later newspaper scraps of his own selection.

Captain Brown died in 1868. The Lincoln Scrap Book passed to his sons William and Benjamin, of Grove Park, Ill., to whom we are indebted for the facts pertaining to its history. In 1900 the book was sold by the Messrs. Brown, to Mr. William H. Lambert of Philadelphia, who possesses the most complete and intelligently arranged Lincoln collection in existence.

It is the unique renown of this book that it is the only one ever written or compiled by Abraham Lincoln. It is reproduced here, as nearly as possible, precisely as it came from his pen and his hand.

J. McCAN DAVIS.

Afterword by J. McCan Davis

After his introductory essay in the *Facsimile*", J. McCan Davis appended a final "Note" which was prefaced by a page stating "A 'Paramount Issue' in 1858."

Davis's "afterword" faced a reprint of a full-page ad published in the Springfield (Illinois) "State Register," a newspaper of the day. Davis said the paper was "the organ of Senator Douglas" and the ad "illustrates the preeminence of 'Negro equality' as an issue in the campaign of 1858 from the Democratic point of view."

Davis's note and the ad are on the following pages.

NOTE.—On the opposite page is the "scare head" of a double-leaded article which the "Illinois State Register" kept standing in its columns for some time previous to the election of 1858. The "State Register" was the organ of Senator Douglas at the State Capital. The article illustrates the preëminence of "negro equality" as an issue in the campaign of 1858, from the Democratic point of view.　　　　　　　J. McC. D.

PEOPLE OF SANGAMON!

REMEMBER

A VOTE FOR COOK AND BROWN

IS A VOTE FOR

LINCOLN AND NEGRO
EQUALITY!

VOTE FOR

BARRET and SHORT

AND SUSTAIN

DOUGLAS

AND

POPULAR RIGHTS.

William H. Lambert

The 1901 Facsimile:
A Behind the Scenes Peek By
Ida M. Tarbell,
William H. Lambert,
George D. Smith and DeWitt Miller

There is much more to the story of the 1901 *Facsimile*'s publication than J. McCan Davis's 16 words in a single sentence at the conclusion of his 11-page "Explanatory Note": "In 1900, the book was sold by the Messrs. Brown to Mr. William H. Lambert of Philadelphia . . . ."

The actual history has been discovered in three extraordinary letters that surfaced in January 2022 in a single copy of the *Facsimile* in the personal library of **William Butts**, owner of Main Street Fine Books & Manuscripts, Galena, Illinois.

This copy, named "Galena" in Butts' hometown's honor, and now in the Abraham Lincoln Presidential Library and Museum, is unique. Of the 3,500 manufactured, this singular book, originally owned by **DeWitt Miller** of Cross River, New York, has on succeeding pages handwritten correspondence to Miller from **Ida M. Tarbell**, **William H. Lambert** and **George D. Smith**. The letters trace the precise publishing history of the *Facsimile*. They are reproduced and transcribed in Appendix D.

The letters clearly reveal that around 1897 or 1898 – the exact date cannot be pinned down – the Brown brothers first offered their 'notebook' to Lambert. *He turned them down.* Why, he does not say. At the same time Tarbell and Davis were separately negotiating with the brothers for the rights to publish Lincoln's notes and clips. They, too, were getting nowhere.

The letters hint at the closeness of the Lincoln devotee community of the late 19th century. Tarbell, Davis, Lambert all knew each other; either personally in the case of Tarbell and Davis who were co-authors of an earlier Lincoln book, or by reputation, regarding Lambert who'd already made a name as a collector.

Undaunted, the brothers went to Smith. Born in 1870, he was 27- or 28-years-of-age and just getting started in the rare book business. They must have mentioned Lambert's demurer. Smith, taking an entrepreneurial leap of faith, met their price and bought the little notebook.[1] He waited a while – perhaps as many as two years – and went back to Lambert who, realizing his mistake and the book's rarity, purchased it – doubtless for far more than the Browns asked. And then, working with Tarbell and Davis – who wrote the introduction – he got it published, likely recouping some or all of his initial purchase cost.

Lambert died in 1912 and Smith, now on commission from Henry E. Huntington, bought the book again, this time for Huntington's nascent San Marino, California, library.

Among the four players in the 1901 *Facsimile*'s story, **Ida M. Tarbell (1857-1944)** was a crusading investigative journalist and polymath who, among her other interests, was an assiduous Lincoln researcher and author.

"Tarbell had been fascinated with Lincoln since she was a seven-year-old girl," one source states, "remembering the news of his assassination and her parents' reaction to it: her father coming home from his shop, her mother burying her 'face in her apron, running into her room sobbing as if her heart would break.'"

Tarbell's Lincoln journalism was spurred, according to Huntington Library scholar Olga Tsapina, when she was engaged by "*McClure's Magazine* [in 1894] to write a documentary biography of Lincoln. Aided by a network of researchers, Tarbell unearthed a mass of new documentary evidence gleaned from newspapers, courthouse records, and private collections."

In the "Galena" copy's letter of February 23, 1901, Tarbell writes she "first heard of [the Lincoln scrapbook's] existence about three years ago [around 1897-1898] in Springfield" but was unable to strike a deal with the [Brown brother] owners.

[1] Smith, unlike historian-collectors Tarbell, Davis or Lambert, got involved in the book for its pecuniary value versus interest in its historical worth.

Later, "after long negotiations Mr. Davis secured for us the right to reproduce the book in fac-simile." She adds "a few months later it was sold to my friend Mr. **[William H.] Lambert [1842 – 1912].**"

Tarbell was proud of her involvement, concluding her letter: "Hoping, my dear Mr. Miller that you will enjoy the fac-simile as much as I have the rather slow task of seeing it brought to the public." [2]

Lambert was a pioneering insurance broker and, later, philanthropist who lived in the Germantown suburb of Philadelphia, Pennsylvania. Training to be a lawyer, he enlisted at age 20 in 1862 as a private and rose through the ranks eventually becoming a Major at the Civil War's end. "His vocation was manager of the Philadelphia agency of the New York Mutual Life Insurance Company, but his avocation was collecting books, autograph letters and manuscripts by and relating to Abraham Lincoln" said one obituary. In this pursuit, he was among the most well-known of Lincoln collectors and attributed his Lincoln success to buying "early."

At one time, Lambert owned the desk and chair that had been in Lincoln's Springfield law office as well as chairs from the White House library. However, according to a contemporary letter, they were lost in a June 15, 1906 home library fire from which fortunately, the *Facsimile* survived because "in accordance with my custom each Summer, these [and other documents] had been removed to safes in the city."

As noted, around 1898 he had the initial opportunity to purchase the book from the Browns. As he somewhat ruefully wrote in his "Galena" note on July 16, 1901: "Probably I could have obtained the book from the Messrs Brown three years ago but for some reason allowed the opportunity to pass."

Recognizing he made a mistake, Lambert writes: "Last fall [in

[2] It was Tarbell's 1924 book *In the Footsteps of the Lincolns* which directly spurred the research leading to the writing of *this* book. In Appendix D are both her notes in the "Galena" edition as well as illustrations of the 1924 book's cover and its key "discovery" pages 360 and 361.

1900] Mr. **George D. Smith [1870-1920]** of New York offered the book and I accepted it promptly. I value it more highly because of its unique personal association with Abraham Lincoln." As to the *Facsimile's* production quality, Lambert wrote: "I consider [it] an excellent reproduction of the original." (His note appears in Appendix D.)

Lambert died in 1912 and his voluminous Lincoln collection was the subject of five separate sales in January 1914. The notebook, lot 477, was snapped up by the same George D. Smith for $2,250, purchasing it as an agent for Henry Huntington. It was described in the auction notice (reprinted in Appendix C,) a copy of which is in the Huntington Library, as "nothing more interesting than this little book could be secured by the collector of historical relics."

Described in a 1959 Grolier Club monograph as "the greatest rare-book dealer of his day" and as a "wily New Yorker" by bibliophile author Nicholas Basbanes in his book *A Gentle Madness,* Smith appears to be the only one of the "Galena" foursome who twice profited from the Lincoln scrapbook. "I bought the original of this book [from the Brown brothers] and sold it to Major W. H. Lambert of Philadelphia who does not want the price he paid mentioned", Smith coyly wrote on Sept. 16, 1901. (See Appendix D.)

Unsaid: At age 28, Smith purchased the original Brown brothers' notebook. Its subsequent sale to Lambert in 1900 may have been the springboard that skyrocketed his career. An example of Smith's rise to affluence as well as his publicity flare; a May 16, 1912 *New York Times* story headlined: "Lamon Lincolniana Bought for $20,000; Famous Autograph Collection Now on Exhibition at G.D. Smith [48 Wall Street basement] Showrooms". Later, Smith moved "uptown" to 547 Fifth Avenue.

To William Butts, noted above, the author is indebted for the following information about **DeWitt Miller (1857-1911)** the original owner of the "Galena" *Facsimile,* whose dogged pursuit of Tarbell, Lambert and Smith gave us their recollections.

One biography of Miller states: "He was fond of association copies, books with presentation notes or corrections in the author's hand, or books that had once been in the library of a famous person." This book clearly fit perfectly into that collecting scheme.

Miller likely purchased the book in early 1901. How or when he encountered Tarbell is unknown. It is even possible he acquired the copy from her. In any case, she penned six leaves of comments on February 23, 1901 in the first blank pages that follow Davis's 'afterword'.

William H. Lambert wrote his three pages several months later – on July 1, 1901. Then, two-and-a half months later, rare book dealer George D. Smith added his single sentence comment on September 16, 1901.

Lastly, in the upper left-hand corner on the page opposite the inside back cover is written lightly in pencil: *"1st edn., with ANSs at back of Ida Tarbell, Wm. H. Lambert & George D. Smith: Important association copy. $200ºº"*. This is shown on page 94. The **unknown** author of this notation is likely a bookseller through whose hands the book passed after its ownership by Miller.

Here is the "Galena" *Facsimile's* provenance:

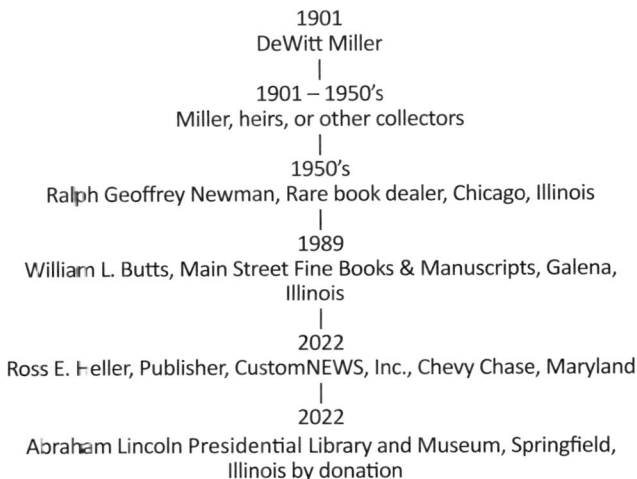

1901
DeWitt Miller
|
1901 – 1950's
Miller, heirs, or other collectors
|
1950's
Ralph Geoffrey Newman, Rare book dealer, Chicago, Illinois
|
1989
William L. Butts, Main Street Fine Books & Manuscripts, Galena, Illinois
|
2022
Ross E. Feller, Publisher, CustomNEWS, Inc., Chevy Chase, Maryland
|
2022
Abraham Lincoln Presidential Library and Museum, Springfield, Illinois by donation

Abraham Lincoln

1st ed., with ANSs
at back of Ida Terbell, Wm.
H. Lambert & George D. Smith.
Important association copy.
$200.00

THE PROPERTY OF
DEWITT MILLER
CROSS RIVER
WESTCHESTER CO.
NEW YORK

Twenty-First
Century

Ida M. Tarbell

Journey's End

The 1901 *Facsimile's* history has been described. But what of *by Abraham Lincoln's* road to publication – 164 years after Lincoln put pen to paper in Springfield, Illinois?

In 1924, late in her career, Ida M. Tarbell wrote a 418-page history-travelogue *In the Footsteps of the Lincolns*. It traces Lincoln's family from his great-great-great-great-grandfather Samuel Lincoln. Since Ms. Tarbell's book covers *all* of Samuel's descendants, it is a while until *our* Abraham – there were others – comes onto the scene. And describing his 1858 run for the Senate, the book briefly ties together Brown, the scrapbook and the *Facsimile*. Of which volume Tarbell writes intriguingly: "it is now a rare document, the edition having been exhausted."

In mid-2021 reading Tarbell's book and seeing the words "*rare document*", a collector's curiosity is piqued. And finding a battered *Facsimile*, an entrepreneurial thought; reprint this long-lost volume. Traced to the Huntington Library, the original was available for scanning. Yet, on opening three gigabytes of data, a surprise; 29 pages of notes, news clips and ephemera added by 1858 campaigner Brown and 1901 editor Davis. No longer a reprint; the project became an entirely new venture.

Then another discovery. Researching Davis, copies of *his* 1909 Lincoln biography were found with Galena, Illinois rare-book dealer, William L. Butts. One Friday afternoon in a *Facsimile*-project phone conversation Butts mentioned his *personal*, non-inventory, *Facsimile*. Which "by the way," he said casually, "I think has some letters in it." Adding "but I can't look now. I have to help my wife pack for a weekend's trip."

A long two-day wait ensued. By whom were the letters written? What did they say? Where did this particular *Facsimile* come from? On Monday Butts provided answers. Dated, descriptive, hand-written correspondence by the *Facsimile's* key players: Tarbell, Lambert and Smith. Letters authoritatively telling the *Facsimile's* publishing history. As well, an extraordinary printed 'note to readers' from the book's publisher McClure & Phillips. And the book itself? Originally owned by turn-of-the-20th-century autograph collector DeWitt Miller of Cross River, New York, about whom Butts had a bit of knowledge.

Butts agreed to sell the unique volume; understanding it would be donated to the Abraham Lincoln Presidential Library and Museum. Thus, the nation's most valuable *Facsimile* has come home to Springfield. And at journey's end, the words of Lincoln, Brown, Davis, Tarbell, Lambert, Smith and publisher McClure & Phillips are available to all in *by Abraham Lincoln: His 1858 Time Capsule*.

Appendices

E Abraham Lincoln

The Huntington Library, San Marino, California

Appendix A

About the 1901 Facsimile's *Manufacture*

Even beyond its content, the *1901 Abraham Lincoln His Book A Facsimile Reproduction of the Original With An Explanatory Note by J. McCan Davis* is a most interesting publication.

First, its size; barely 3" x 6". And then its title page, copyright and 'explanatory notes' begin in the middle of the book after Lincoln's quotes. Most contemporary pagination has such items at the front.

1,500 copies of the 1901 first edition were printed by Mc-Clure Phillips & Co. of New York and re-published in 1903. In 1909 Doubleday, Page & Company printed a third edition.

Part of the *Facsimile's* actual manufacturing process was the inclusion in some first edition copies of a most unusual four-folded "Publisher's Note on the Making of the Lincoln: His Book." It describes "unprecedent difficulties" that "again and again during the progress of the work, and more particularly during its delays, it was declared by the workman to be impossible on any terms."

Getting into the weeds, the note states: "Usually, of course, a book which is to be imitated [in facsimile] is taken to pieces, but the Lincoln book must not only not be dismembered, it must be handled with the greatest care."

The note also describes "the leather for the [1901] binding was especially made. Care was taken to have its inner side yellow, so that when abrasions were made later, the time-worn look of the original should be duplicated." Even the typeface is noted; chosen "for its likeness to a kind popular in country newspaper offices at the time Mr. Lincoln compiled the book." Both sides of the "Publisher's Note" can be found below.

The initial printing of the book had both a 'standard' and a 'deluxe' edition; the latter distinguished by being enclosed in a slipcase. This 'deluxe' slipcase had the words ABRAHAM LINCOLN: HIS BOOK pasted on the front and spine. The slipcase is of a 'pebbly' texture with a semi-circular die cut for ease of removing the book itself. Also on the following pages is an illustration of the "deluxe edition" slipcase's cover and spine.

Interestingly the 1901 'deluxe' edition had TWO hard covers. One, might be considered the book's 'jacket' though removable and without printing. The other was the actual bound cover. This cover is dark brown in color with a leather-like texture. (The 1909 Doubleday, Page & Company edition had a black leather-like cover.)

This Appendix includes both sides of the Publisher's note, 1901 *Facsimile* cover page; 1901 copyright page and the 1901 book's deluxe slipcase cover and spine.

A Publisher's Note on the Making of the Lincoln: His Book.

The making of such a fac-simile as this is only possible through photography. Again and again during the progress of the work, and more particularly during its delays, it was declared by the workman to be impossible on any terms. The expert who adopted the half-tone process to fac-simile reproduction and made the first photographic successes therein was in charge of the work; but he had unprecedented difficulties to contend with. Usually, of course, a book which is to be imitated is taken to pieces, but the Lincoln book must not only not be dismembered, it must be handled with the greatest care. In photographing the pages of an open book widths of margins must differ according to what pages were exposed,—a closely bound book does not open so wide in the middle as at its first or last pages. In addition, gelatine plates have most irregular ways of shrinking. This shrinkage makes little difference when pages are photographed on a larger surface, but when the plates themselves must make the pages, then scores of trials are necessary, sometimes, to get one the proper size. Consequently this especial feat is rarely attempted, and the Lincoln note-book is an achievement as unusual as it is successful. The leather for the binding was especially made for the purpose. Care was taken to have its inner side yellow, so that when abrasions were made later, the time-worn look of the original should be duplicated. When it came to making these abrasions sand-paper was first tried, but the result was too scratchy; finally, by rubbing between boards, a perfectly time-worn appearance was at last obtained.

The type for Mr. Davis' note was chosen for its likeness to a kind popular in country newspaper offices at the time Mr. Lincoln compiled the book.

Publisher's note Side 1

Abraham Lincoln

THIS IS THE
MARK OF McCLURE
PHILLIPS & CO.

IT MEANS THE
BEST IN BOOKS

ABRAHAM
LINCOLN

HIS BOOK

A FACSIMILE REPRODUC-
TION OF THE ORIGINAL

WITH AN

EXPLANATORY NOTE

BY

J. McCAN DAVIS

NEW YORK:
McCLURE, PHILLIPS & CO.
1901

Publisher's note Side 2

Appendix A

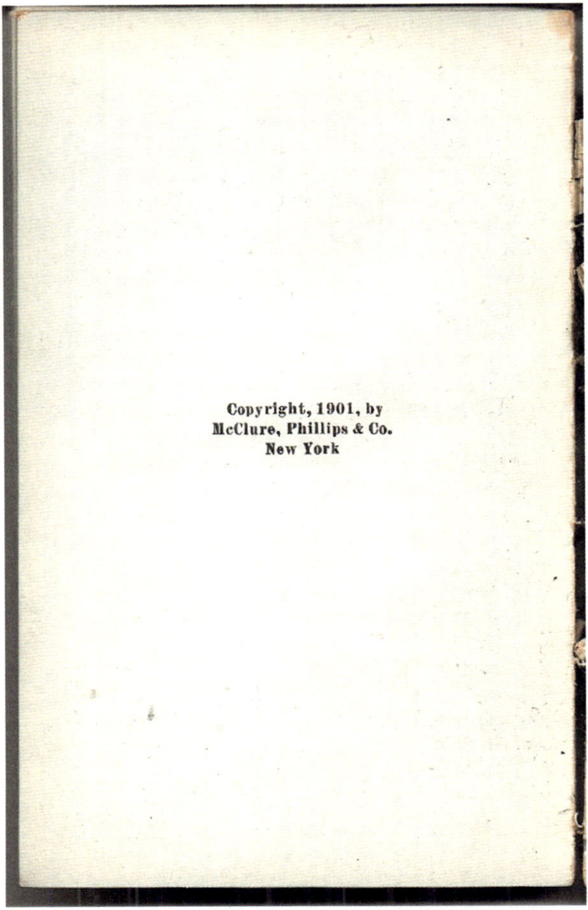

Copyright, 1901, by
McClure, Phillips & Co.
New York

1901 copyright page

Abraham Lincoln

1901 *Facsimile* cover

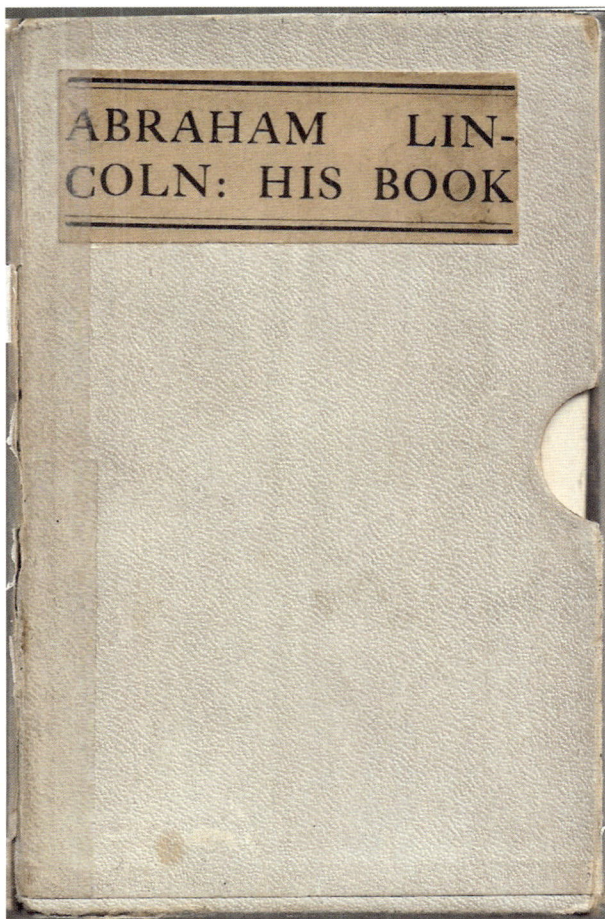

1901 *Facsimile* deluxe slipcase cover

1901 *Facsimile* deluxe slipcase spine

Appendix B

News Clippings Added by James N. Brown

James N. Brown not only used Lincoln's 'scrapbook' when campaigning in 1858, but also added his own news clippings-some as late as 1864.

They are reproduced here, in the same order as in the book located at the Huntington Library. Each clip is annotated by its Huntington Library document page number.

is poor! The Richmond *Enquirer*, one of Douglas' leading Southern organs, does not mince its words. It says:—

"*Make the laboring man the slave of one man,* instead of the slave of society, and he would be far better off.

"Two hundred years of labor have made laborers a *pauper banditti. Free society has failed,* and that which is *not free must be substituted.*

"*Free society is a monstrous abortion,* and slavery the healthy, beautiful and natural being which they are trying unconsciously to adopt.

"*The slaves are governed far better than the free laborers of the North are governed.* Our negroes are not only better off as to physical comfort than free laborers, but *their moral condition is better.*

"We do not adopt the theory that Ham was the ancestor of the negro race. The Jewish slaves were not negroes; and to confine the jurisdiction of slavery to that race would be to weaken its scriptural authority, for we read of no negro slavery in ancient times. *Slavery, black or white, is necessary.*

"Nature has made the *weak in mind and body slaves.* * * * *The wise and virtuous, the brave, the strong in mind or body are born to command* * * * *Men are not born entitled to equal rights.* It would be far nearer the truth to say that *some were born with saddles on their backs, and others booted and spurred to ride them; and the riding does them good. They need the whip, the reins, the spur.* * * *Life and liberty are not inalienable.* * * *The Declaration of Independence is exuberantly false and fallacious.*"

Read, also, the following from the Charleston *Standard,* another organ of the same ilk:

' *Slavery is the natural and normal condition of the laboring man, whether WHITE or black,* The great evil of Northern *free society* is, that it is burdened with a *servile* class of *mechanics and laborers,* unfit for self-government, and yet clothed with the attributes and the powers of citizens. Master and slave is a relation in society as necessary as that of a parent and child, and the Northern States will have yet to introduce it. Their theory of free government is a delusion.

"The truth is, that all men are not born equal

mssHM2144_p 30a

LARGEST AND MOST ELEGANT

ing the

would respectfully inform the ladies of this City and
ty and all the surrounding counties, that we are now

LET US FRIGHTEN THEM.—This is virtually
the language of a portion of the Breckinridge
party at the South, spoken with reference to
the Republicans. As an instance, we copy
the following deliberate statement from the
Charleston *Mercury's* review of the political
aspects of the times, and bespeak for it the
candid attention of all our readers:

The Presidential election turns upon a single fact. If the Northern people believe that
the Southern people will dissolve their connection with them, should the Black Republican party succeed in electing Lincoln to the
Presidency—Lincoln *will be defeated*. Should
they, on the contrary, believe that the Southern people will submit to Black Republican
domination, by the election of Lincoln to the
Presidency—Lincoln *will be elected*.

Abraham Lincoln

Popular Sovereignty.

In addressing a New England audience the other day, Mr. Douglas as he has often before, asked why a citizen, emigrating from Iowa to Kansas, should lose his right of self-government on the ferry-boat while crossing the Missouri River. The object of this question was to leave the impression on the minds of his hearers that what he vauntingly styles "my great principle," is intended to confer, and really does confer, the same right of self-government upon the citizens of the Territories which are enjoyed by the citizens of the States. Let us see whether the facts will warrant the assumption.

The citizens of our respective State governments enjoy certain rights, the possession of which constitutes State sovereignty—or popular sovereignty in the States. These rights pertain (1) to entire control of State affairs: and (2) to a voice, proportionate to population, in the affairs of the general government. Under the first the following may be enumerated.

1. The right to establish a Fundamental Law.

2. The right to elect a Governor; to define his duties, to limit his power, and to determine his tenure of office.

3. The right to make all laws needful for the security and well-being of society.

4. The right to establish courts and to elect a Judiciary.

Under the second class of rights are the following :

1. An equal voice with each of the other States in the United States Senate.

2. A representation in the United States House of Representatives, proportioned to population.

mssHM2144_p31a

population.

3. A voice in the election of President of
the United States, corresponding with the
representation of the States respectively in
Congress.

Now, when Douglas asks the question,
why a citizen of Iowa, emigrating to Kansas,
should lose his right to self-government,
while, crossing the Missouri River, he embraces all that is included in the above, (for
they are rights belonging to every citizen of
Iowa,) and he seeks to convey the idea that,
under his Kansas bill, all these rights are
guarranteed to the citizens of Kansas but
what is the fact ?

1. The Kansas bill is the fundamental law
of Kansas, and in the framing of it the citizens of Kansas had no more voice than the
supjects of the Tycoon.

2. The Govornor of Kansas is appointed
by the President of the United States, holds
office at his pleasure, and is responsible to
him alone for his acts.

3. The people of Kansas are permitted
to elect their Legislature; but the Governor,
(the tool of the President) is clothed with the
veto power, and through it, is made equal to
two-thirds of the Legislature.

4. The people of Kansas are not allowed
to establish courts, and elect Judges and other
officers. The former is done by congress, and
the president appoints the latter.

5. The people of Kansas have no voice in
the United States Senate.

6. The people of Kansas are graciously allowed to send one delegate to the House of Representatives; *but he is carefully excluded
from voting.*

7. The people of Kansas have no voice in the election of President.

Now, then, the next time Mr. Douglas asks why a citizen of a State, in passing into a Territory, should lose his right to self-government on crossing the boundary between the two, let some one put a question to him. Let him be asked, Why did you Mr. Douglas, in framing the Kansas Nebraska bill, provide that he should lose that right? Why did you take away from him the right to frame his own fundamental law—the right to elect a Governor—the right to have a Legislature that cannot be overridden by a creature of the President—the right to establish his own courts and elect his own judges and other officers—the right to a voice in the United States Senate—the right to a vote in the House of Representatives—the right to vote for President of the United States? Why did you take all the rights away from these people of Kansas, Mr. Douglas? You say that in the act of crossing the boundary line which separates a State from a Territory, a fit him for self-government. Then why did you, Mr. Douglas, put in your bill those provisions which strip him almost wholly of that right? Is not, in fact, all this zeal of yours, Mr. Douglas, in behalf of "the sacred right of self government," merely a cloak and a blind under which you hope to force slavery into the Territories and yourself into the Presidency? Is there any right of self-government, Mr Douglas, in your Kansas Nebraska bill, not to be found in all other Territorial bills which Congress has adopted, except the right (by aid of the Dred scott decision) to carry slaves into the Territory? And is not that the first and the last, the beginning and the end of the "great principle?"—*Pres-and Tribune.*

"We are satisfied that no wh) reads attentively the page in Peter's Reports, to which we have referred, can suppose that the Court meant in that case to say that Congress has a right to prohibit a citizen of the United States from taking *any* property which he lawfully held into a territory of the United States. And if Congress itself cannot do this—if it is beyond the powers conferred on the Federal Government—it will be admitted, we presume, THAT IT COULD NOT AUTHORIZE A TERRITORIAL GOVERNMENT TO EXERCISE THEM. And if the Constitution recognizes the right of property of the master in a slave, and makes no distinction between that description of property and other property owned by a citizen, no tribunal, acting under the authority of the United States, whether it be LEGISLATIVE, executive or judicial, has a right to draw such a distinction, or deny to it the benefit of the provisions and guarantees which have been provided for the protection of private property against the encroachment of the Government."—[Dred Scott decision, delivered by Chief Justice Taney, pp. 451.

Following we copy the clause from the bill o Toombs requiring the submission, and that of Mr. Douglas with the clause struck out:

TOOMBS' BILL.	DOUGLAS' BILL.
13th Sec. of the Toombs' Bill—"That the following propositions be, and the same are hereby, offered to the said Convention of the people of Kansas, when formed, for their free acceptance or rejection, which, if accepted by the Convention, AND RATIFIED BY THE PEOPLE AT THE ELECTION FOR THE ADOPTION OF THE CONSTITUTION, shall be obligatory on the United States, and upon the said State of Kansas, etc."	19th Section of Douglas' amended Bill—"That the following propositions be, and the same are hereby offered to the said Convention of the people of Kansas, for their free acceptance or rejection, which, IF ACCEPTED BY THE CONVENTION, shall be obligatory upon the United States and upon the said State of Kansas," etc.

It will be seen, by comparing the phraseology of the above two sections, that the words, "ratified by the people at the election for the adoption of the Constitution," in Toombs' Bill, are stricken out of Douglas' amended Bill, and Mr. Douglas, in reporting the amended Bill, stated that he himself made the alteration."

...now call your attention.

I start out by showing the absolute contradictions of Mr. Douglas himself. I have before me a speech made by him at Concord, New Hampshire, since he was nominated for the Presidency, and published in the Missouri *Republican*. I shall read a single sentence from that speech, as follows:

"I hold that every political community, State and Territory alike, has, under our system of government, the right to govern itself in all things that are local and domestic."

In his *Harper Magazine* article he said that the State of Pennsylvania and the Territory of Kansas were subordinate to the Constitution "in the same measure, and to the same extent," thus placing States and Territories on the same footing. These are clear propositions. Now suppose I show that this doctrine has been denied, repudiated and spit upon by the very man who advanced it. [Cheers and cries of "good, good."] What then? Is a man fit to be President who contradicts himself? who swallows his own words?

I will now read what Mr. Douglas said in one of his articles in reply to Judge Black. This is his language:

"I have never said or thought that our Territories were sovereign political communities, or even limited sovereignties like the States of this Union."

[Great and prolonged cheering.] You, Mr. Douglas, never said or thought any such thing! And yet you have the brazen face—the impudence to go before the American people and tell them, that the people of a Territory, like those of a State, have the right to manage all their domestic concerns for themselves! [Applause.] Now, I want to see what this consistent man says of popular sovereignty, to which he once boasted that he had been devoting his life for many years. [Laughter and cheers.] Remember, these are not my words—they are the words of a man who has devoted his life to the advocacy of this great principle! He says:

"Sovereign States have the right to make their own Constitutions and establish their own governments, and alter and change the same at pleasure. I have never claimed these powers for the Territories, nor have I ever failed to resist such claim when set up by others."

Why, Mr. Douglas has resisted sovereignty in a Territory when anybody else has set it up...

m͵ssHM2144_p34

laughter and cheers.] What I present now does not depend on my statement. In his New Orleans speech, Mr. Douglas said:

"I have been repeatedly asked, here and elsewhere, what I meant by Popular Sovereignty in the Territories. My answer is, that I mean the right of the people to form their own institutions, as guaranteed in the Kansas-Nebraska Bill."

Mark the language: he means by Popular Sovereignty the right of the people to form their own institutions as guaranteed in the Kansas-Nebraska Bill. What did he say in the speech he made a few days ago? He says in New Hampshire:

"The Republican tells you that the moment a citizen of New Hampshire (who possesses the inherent right of self-government so long as he stays here) crosses a State line, and enters a Territory of the United States, he forfeits the right. [Ironical cheers.] Is it true that a citizen of New Hampshire forfeits his inalienable right of self-government when he moves to a Territory? ["No, sir-ee," and laughter.] What provision of the Constitution of the United States works that forfeiture? ["None."] Then upon what ground is it that an American citizen is deprived of his rights when he goes into a Territory under the constitution and the American flag?—Will it be said that the people of the Territories are not capable of self-government? Who are the people of the Territories? Where did they come from? Many of them are your sons, your brothers, who have left the granite hills of their native State and went to Kansas. They were capable of self government, were they not, when they left home? When did they lose the capacity to govern themselves? [Laughter and cheers.] Were they any less capable of self-government after they got to Kansas than they were when they started?—Did they lose all their senses and intelligence and the virtue they possessed while on the ferry boat crossing the Missouri river? [Laughter.] Where and when I ask, did the native born citizen, who was capable of self-government when he started, lose that capacity?

If I now

party — and that party exist to this day and are and ever have been for disunion —

I will call your attention to one other thing. He said in his Concord speech:

"Having heard the Republican party pledge themselves so often against the admission of any more slave States into the Union, it did rejoice me when I saw every man in the Senate and every man in the House voting to allow Kansas to come in as a slave State, if the people should desire it."

[Laughter and cheers.]

"I would say that in all cases where there are outrages upon our flag and citizens and property, demanding instant redress, not admitting of delay, he President may use the army and navy to enforce such redress, and then report the facts to Congress. I introduced a bill of that kind last year, during the last session of Congress, in order to confer its authority upon the President, not with reference to any case then pending, but as a general rule. I desire the President of the United States to have as much authority to protect American citizens, American property, and the American flag abroad, as the executive of every other civilized nation on earth possesses."

He then argued that fewer outrages would be committed on our rights:—

"When it is known that the Executive has the same authority outside of the United States to redress these outrages that the British Premier, or *the French Emperor,* or the head of any other Nation, possesses."

Now, I would like to ask an American audience, anywhere, whether they are for vesting in the President of the United States the same authority in regard to redressing injuries committed by the foreign nations that is possessed by the Emperor of the French? ["No," "no."] Why did the men who made your Constitution so carefully insert in it the clause prohibiting the Executive from declaring war? and why did they reserve that power to Congress? It was for your protection against the hasty acts of some ambitious Executive. Yet Mr. Douglas introduced a bill which practically placed this high power in the hands of the Executive alone, and that, too, in the very teeth of the Constitution itself.

mssHM2144_p36a

Douglas plays the political thimble-rig game equal to the most expert of blacklegs. In Pennsylvania and New Jersey, where a tariff is popular, Douglas in one of his speeches said :

Now, I suppose there are none of us who are not satisfied that, on the subject of the tariff, there ought to be material changes. How is it? The Collectors of your ports are becoming rich; your government is becoming poor. Is it not time that we should establish a home valuation upon every article that is brought into the country, so that we may prevent fraud? Is it not time that we should discuss and investigate whether, upon many articles, it is not our wise and just policy to-day to levy specific duties, to the end that honest revenue may be collected, and that we may have the great interests of the country protected. [Applause.]

The Baltimore Platform, on which Douglas was nominated, reiterated the Cincinnati Platform, and the latter especially condemned protection to Northern manufactures, on the ground that it was cherishing the interests of one section at the expense of another; and that Platform expressly declared that "no more revenue ought to be raised than is required to defray the necessary expenses of the government."

At Washington — before his Southern masters—Douglas said:

"Bear in mind that these questions touching the right of property in slaves was referred to the Territorial Courts with right of appeal to Supreme Court. When that case shall arise and the Court pronounce its judgment, it will be binding, and the army, navy, and militia must be used to carry it into effect."

And in Illinois, Douglas—before the people—said:

"It matters not what way the Supreme Court may decide the question, the people have control of it, for the reason that slavery cannot exist a day or an hour anywhere, unless it is supported by local police regulations; these police regulations can only be established by a local Legislature, and if the people are opposed to slavery they can elect representatives to that body who will, by unfriendly legislation, effectually prevent the introduction of it into their midst."

And, as with the thimble and the little joker, so with Douglas—"Now you see it, and now you don't."

Douglas' Portrait—By Himself.

These two brief extracts from speeches of S. A. Douglas, give an admirable and correct view of his real political character—that of a low, designing, tricky demagogue, who has no principles to guide him, and no policy except what for the moment promises the most advantage to himself:

From Douglas' Speech, at Springfield, Ills., in 1849.—All the evidences of public opinion at that day seemed to indicate that this (the Missouri) Compromise had become canonized in the hearts of the American people as a sacred thing which no ruthless hand would ever be reckless enough to disturb.

From Douglas' Speech at Providence, R. I., Aug. 3, 1860.—My friend over there—friend or enemy as the case may be—wants to know something about the Missouri Compromise [Cheers.] I have not the slightest objection to telling him all he desires to know upon that question. *I brought in the bill to repeal the Missouri Restriction.*

Mr Short said that I said a negro in africa was as good as a negro in africa — Now I tell you what I did say —

120

mssHM2144_p38a

WHAT POPULAR SOVEREIGNTY HAS DONE.

Mr. Douglas Called to the Witness Stand.

READ! READ!! READ!!!

[From Mr. Douglas' Speech in the Senate, May 16, 1860.]

But, we are told that the necessary result of this doctrine of non-intervention, which gentlemen, by way of throwing ridicule upon, call squatter sovereignty, is to deprive the South of all participation in what they call the common Territories of the United States. That was the ground on which the Senator from Mississippi [Mr. Davis] predicated his opposition to the compromise measures of 1840. He regarded a refusal to repeal the Mexican law as equivalent to the Wilmot proviso; a refusal to deny to a Territorial Legislature the right to exclude slavery as equivalent to an exclusion. He believed at that time that this doctrine did amount to a denial of Southern rights; and he told the people of Mississippi so; but they doubted it. Now, let us see how far his predictions and suppositions have been verified. I infer that he told the people so, for as he makes it a charge in his bill of indictment against me, that I am hostile to Southern rights, because I gave those votes.

Now, what has been the result? My views were incorporated into the compromise measure of 1850, and his were rejected. Has the South been excluded from all the territory acquired from Mexico? What says the bill from the House of Representatives now on your table, repealing the slave code in New Mexico established by the people themselves? IT IS PART OF THE HISTORY OF THE COUNTRY THAT UNDER THIS DOCTRINE OF NON-INTERVENTION, THIS DOCTRINE THAT YOU DELIGHT TO CALL SQUATTER SOVEREIGNTY, THE PEOPLE OF NEW MEXICO HAVE INTRODUCED AND PROTECTED SLAVERY IN THE WHOLE OF THAT TERRITORY. UNDER THIS DOCTRINE, THEY HAVE CONVERTED A TRACT OF FREE TERRITORY INTO SLAVE TERRITORY, MORE THAN FIVE TIMES THE SIZE OF THE STATE OF NEW YORK. UNDER THIS DOCTRINE, SLAVERY HAS BEEN EXTENDED FROM THE RIO GRANDE TO THE GULF OF CALIFORNIA, AND FROM THE LINE OF THE REPUBLIC OF MEXICO, NOT ONLY UP TO 36 DEG. 30 MIN. BUT UP TO 38 DEG.—GIVING YOU A DEGREE AND A HALF MORE SLAVE TERRITORY THAN YOU EVER CLAIMED. In 1848 and 1849 and 1850 you only asked to have the line of 36 deg. 30 min. The Nashville Convention fixed that as its ultimatum. I offered it in the Senate in August, 1848, and it was adopted here but rejected in the House of Representatives. You asked only up to 36 deg. 30 min., AND NON-INTERVENTION HAS GIVEN YOU SLAVE TERRITORY UP TO 38 DEG., A DEGREE AND A HALF MORE THAN YOU ASKED; and yet you say that this is a sacrifice of Southern rights?

E Abraham Lincoln

mssHM2144_p38a

These are the fruits of this principle which the Senator from Mississippi regards as hostile to the rights of the South.—Where did you ever get any other fruits that were more palatable to your tastes or more refreshing to your strength? WHAT OTHER INCH OF FREE TERRITORY HAS BEEN CONVERTED INTO SLAVE TERRITORY ON THE AMERICAN CONTINENT, SINCE THE REVOLUTION, EXCEPT IN NEW MEXICO AND ARIZONIA, UNDER THE PRINCIPLE OF NON-INTERVENTION affirmed at Charleston. If it be true that this principle of non-intervention has conferred upon you all that immense teritory; has protected slavery in that comparatively northern and cold region where you did not expect it to go, cannot you trust the same principle further South when you come to acquire additional teritory from Mexico? If it be true this principle of non-intervention has given to slavery all New Mexico, which was surrounded on nearly every side by free territory, will not the same principle protect you in the northern States of Mexico when they are acquired, since they are now surrounded by slave territory; are several hundred miles further South; have many degrees of greater heat; and have a climate and soil adapted to Southern products? ARE YOU NOT SATISFIED WITH THESE PRACTICAL RESULTS?

122

mssHM2144_p39a

In 1844 Don Morrison offered the following Resolution in the House of Representatives, which may be found on page 167 of the House Journal of that year:

Mr. Morrison moved to amend the motion made by Mr. Hicks, by adding the following, viz: "With *instructions* to inquire particularly into the expediency of *repealing all that part of an Act entitled 'An Act respecting free negroes, mulattoes, servants and slaves,' that prohibits the marriage of the petitioners with ladies of color*, and that they report by bill or otherwise."

Mr. Logan moved to lay this proposed amendment on the table, which was agreed to by yeas and nays, Yates voting in the affirmative, as did also *Mr. Ross.*

So the patriotic and immaculate old Whig, Don Morrison, goes in for marriage and amalgamation with *ladies of color!!* Hurrah for Don! Hurrah for Douglas!!!

Again, Don, in 1849, in the Senate of Illinois, offered the following Resolution for the repeal of all the *main parts* of the "Black Laws," which resolution is found on page 214 of the Senate Journal of 1849.

Mr. Morrison, on leave, offered for adoption the following resolution:

Resolved, That the Committee on the Judiciary be required to report a bill repealing so much of chapter seventy-four, revised laws, as is inapplicable to our condition under the new constitution, and its abolition of indentured servitude or slavery:

Which under the rules lies over one day.

On motion of Mr. Morrison,

The rule was dispensed with, and the resolution read,

And the motion being upon the adoption of the resolution, it was decided in the negative.

Now "chapter 74 of the Revised Laws," is the very chapter that contains *all* the *Black Laws* of Illinois, and Don wanted it mainly repealed!! Thus while Yates did *not* vote to repeal the Black Laws, Don Morrison *did*!! So Hurrah for *Don*, Douglas and the Mulatto Democracy!!!

Finally, in 1849, on the 8th of January, Don Morrison and Joel A. Matteson, then members of the State Senate, both voted for the following resolution which passed and which may be found on page 38 of the Senate Journal of 1849.

Mr. Plato offered for adoption the following resolution:

Resolved by the Senate of the State of Illinois, the House of Representatives concurring therein, That our Senators in Congress be instructed, and our representatives requested, to use all honorable means in their power to procure the enactment of such laws by Congress for the government of the countries or territories of the United States, acquired by treaty of peace, friendship, limits and settlement, with the Republic of Mexico, concluded February 2nd, A. D. 1848, as shall contain the express declaration, that there shall be neither slavery nor involuntary servitude in said territories, otherwise than in the punishment of crimes, whereof the party shall have been duly convicted.

Don Morrison also on the 9th day of January 1849 offered in the Senate the following resolution:

mssHM2144_p39a

Resolved, That his excellency, the govenor, be requested to transmit to each of our senators and representatives in congress, a copy of the joint resolution passed this day, instructing our senators, and requesting our representatives in congress, to oppose the formation of any government over the territories of California and New Mexico, which does not positively prohibit the introduction of slavery or involuntary servitude into said territories.

Hurrah for Don Morrison, Congressional Intervention and Squatter Sovereignty! and "nigger" Equality!! amalgamation, and Bogus *Old Line Whiggery!!!*

Lastly on the 4th of January 1855, Don Morrison in the Senate of Illinois, offered the following Resolution condemning the Nebraska Bill and the repeal the Missouri Compromise.

Mr. Morrison, on leave, offered the following resolutions, which, under the rule, lie over one day:

Resolved by the Senate, the House of Representatives concurring herein: That the General Assembly of the State of Illinois most emphatically disapproves of the repeal of the clause prohibiting of slavery, which was contained in the act admitting Missouri as one of the States of this Union, and our senators in congress are hereby instructed, and our representatives requested, to give their earnest support to the restoration of the said clause prohibiting slavery in the territories of Kansas and Nebraska.

Resolved, the govenor be requested to transmit a copy of these resolutions to our senators and representatives in congress.

Verily, is not Don Morrison worse than Lovejoy or Giddings?

Herschel V. Johnson, candidate for Vice Pres
ident on the ticket with Mr. Douglas, says:

"Few, at the South, deny the *power of Congress* to pass
laws for the *protection* of slave property in the Territories—
I CERTAINLY DO NOT."

* * * * * * * * * *

"I believe that *it is the right of the South to demand* and
the *duty of Congress to extend protection to persons and
property of every kind (including Slavery) in the Territories during their Territorial state.* This is no new opinion.
I advocated the doctrine as far back as 1848 in the Senate of
the United States. If you have any curiosity to see the argument, I refer you to my speech on the Oregon bill, delivered 7th of July of that year, and reported in the Congressional Globe. *How unjust*, therefore, are the insinuations
with which you intersperse and interlard your editorial comments that all are in favor of *"Squatter Sovereignty"* who
happen not to agree with the seceders from the Charleston
Convention! I REPEL THE INSINUATION SO FAR AS IT
MAY BE INTENDED TO APPLY TO ME, COME FROM
WHAT QUARTER IT MAY, AND PLEAD MY OWN REC-
ORD IN VINDICATION."

"Property of all kinds, *slaves as well as any other,* stands
upon the same constitutional basis, and subject *to like principles of recognition* and PROTECTION *in the* LEGISLA-
TIVE, *Judicial and Executive departments of the General
Government.*"—H. V. *Johnson at Rome, Ga.*

Such are the opinions of Messrs. Douglas and
Johnson in denunciation of popular sovereignty.
The platform they stand upon is equally em-
phatic against popular sovereignty and in favor
of Supreme Court Sovereignty. Here is the
new Baltimore plank:

RESOLUTION OF BALTIMORE DOUGLAS CONVENTION.

"*Resolved,* That it is in accordance with the Cincinnati
platform, that during the existence of Territorial Governments the *measure of restriction,* whatever it may be, imposed by the Federal Constitution *on the power of the Territorial Legislature* over the subject of the *domestic relations,*
as the same *has been or shall hereafter be* finally DETER-
MINED BY THE SUPREME COURT of the United States,
should be respected by all good citizens and ENFORCED *with
promptness and fidelity* by EVERY BRANCH *of the General Government.*

This Supreme Court plank which takes the
vital spark out of all there was left of the "great
principle of popular sovereignty" has been
directly indorsed by Mr. Douglas in his letter of
acceptance of the nomination. By the terms of
this resolution, he not only adopts the Dred
Scott decision, but also the next decision which
"*shall hereafter be*" made by the Supreme
Court, which will carry slavery not only into

PEACE.

When two nations at war begin seriously to talk peace, especially after each has suffered as the north and south have suffered during this horrible war, peace is usually not distant. And it now seems to be certain that the two governments of Richmond and Washington are seriously, though informally, taking the preliminary steps towards a settlement of our difficulties. Were a a democratic administration now in power at Washington, we might safely predict a peace in twenty days. But with a sectional party controlling the government, founded and built up on a spirit of hostility towards every slaveholding state of this Union, the prospect for returning peace and prosperity is not so bright.

But the people of the United States will not allow Mr. Lincoln and his abominable party prejudices to stand in the way of this speedy termination of our difficulties. A majority of the people are no more in favor of continuing the war for the complete abolition of slavery, than they were in the first place of taking up arms for that purpose ; and if Jeff. Davis and his associate rebels are willing to come back to the Union on the conditions named in our dispatches, wo betide the men who stand in the way of their return.

No right thinking and patriotic citizen can take exception to the following conditions of peace, said to be those offered by the rebels themselves :

1st. All negroes which have been actually freed by war, to be secured in such freedom.
2d. All negroes at present held as slaves, to remain so.
3d. The war debt of both parties to be paid by the United States.
4th. The old doctrine of state rights to be recognized in reconstructing the Union.

We shall see if Mr. Lincoln and the abolition party dare to refuse the country a restored Union on these eminently fair and favorable conditions. If he does dare refuse such conditions, the democratic party will make them their platform, upon they will sweep every state in the Union which is allowed a vote.

We congratulate the country that peace is not far off.

Daily State Register.

"To Whom it May Concern."

Abraham Lincoln, of March 4th, 1861, and Abraham Lincoln, of July 18th, 1864, cut the following figure:

LINCOLN'S INAUGURAL, MARCH 4, 1861

I declare that I have no purpose, DIRECTLY OR INDIRECTLY, to interfere with the institution of slavery in the states where it exists. I believe I have NO LAWFUL RIGHT TO DO SO, and have NO INCLINATION TO DO SO. * * The RIGHT of each state to order and control its own domestic institutions according its own judgment EXCLUSIVELY, is ESSEN- to the balance of pow- which the perfection ENDURANCE of our fabric depend.

ABRAHAM LINCOLN.

LINCOLN TO THE REBEL COMMISSIONERS, JULY 18TH, 1864.

Any proposition which embraces the restoration of peace, the integrity of the whole Union, and THE ABANDONMENT OF SLAVERY, and comes by and with an authority that can control the armies now at war with the United States, will be received and considered by the executive government of the United States, and will be met by liberal terms on substantial and collateral points; and the bearer or bearers thereof shall have conduct both ways.

ABRAHAM LINCOLN.

mssHM2144_p43a

Another Federal Defeat.

We noted, at the time, the infamous attack of Gen. Burbridge upon the right of electoral franchise in Kentucky by ordering the name of the democratic candidate for appellate judge, Alvin Duvall, to be stricken from the poll-books, and the arrest of many leading democrats. This atrocious order was issued but three or four days before the election, and was intended to secure the "election" of Benton, the abolition candidate. No more outrageous and despicable an assault upon the people's liberties and the constitution of the country has been perpetrated, even by minions of this despicable administration. But the people of Kentucky were not thus to be baffled. At the eleventh hour they brought out another candidate, Mr. Robinson, whom they triumphantly elected. One of the flunkey papers of that noble old state thinks Duvall might as well have been suffered to continue as a candidate. It thus bewails the fate of its candidate:

"The vote of Mr. Benton is smaller than we supposed it would be, even of the small number polled. It is needless to make excuses; the thing is over. And the professed Union men, who used the order of Gen. Burbridge, excluding the name of Judge Duvall from the poll-books, as the basis of appeals that the military were taking away the citizens' rights and destroying the freedom of elections, and thus aroused prejudices against Mr. Benton, may enjoy all the honor they can derive from the recollection of it."

It seems, therefore, that even a despicable general, who lends himself to a despicable and infamous attempt to subvert the right of the people to govern themselves, cannot succeed when the people are determined not to be enslaved. For this let every patriot take courage. As in Kentucky, let every similar atrocity recoil upon the heads of its perpetrators.

The *Boston Traveller gives currency to some* very extraordinary statements respecting the army of the Potomac. It says that the private soldiers have given their officers quietly to understand that they must not expect them to assault impregnable earthworks hereafter; that the campaign so far has been one of useless butchery, in which no regard has been paid to the lives of the troops. This same paper hints, as did the *Tribune* the other day, that the reason the colored soldiers were given the post of honor at Petersburg was because the white troops were indisposed to make the assault. Of course we entirely discredit these rumors of insubordination; but it is probably true that in the army, as well as out of it, there is a feeling that many, very many, valuable lives have been lost without any apparent advantage being gained.

The Rochester *Democrat*, another republican journal, states that there is a great deal of dissatisfaction in the army, and that an unusual number of resignations of officers has been tendered, among whom are five generals. The Boston *Advertiser* also alludes to rumors it has heard to the same effect. All this is calculated to add to the despondency of the country; but we sincerely hope matters are not so bad as they are represented to be.

———————

WHAT should we learn from our repulse at Petersburg? We should learn that the government needs five hundred thousand men.

What should we learn from the invasion of Pennsylvania? We should learn that the government needs five hundred thousand men.

What should we learn from General Sherman's pause before Atlanta? We should learn that the government needs five hundred thousand men.—*Chicago Journal.*

And what, if the government gets these five hundred thousand men, does the history of the last three years teach us that it would do with them?

We should learn that it will kill them off in the course of six months in the attempt to make the rebbls "abandon slavery."

Appendix C

The Huntington Library: A Personal Reflection

The original Lincoln notebook (which New York rare-book dealer George D. Smith purchased at the auction sale of William H. Lambert's estate on commission from Henry E. Huntington) is now part of the permanent collection of the Huntington Library, San Marino, California.

The book can be viewed by appointment in the Ahmanson rare book reading room within the Huntington's Munger Research Center.

It should come as no surprise the original 'scrapbook' closely resembles its 1901 *Facsimile* (or vice versa.) The *Facsimile's* publisher/manufacturer did an exceptionally good job, given the technology of the times, in making a close copy of Lincoln's book. This is true even to the worn look of the *Facsimile* book's cover.

Huntington Research Librarian Olga Tsapina commented on the scrapbook's darkened first two pages compared to the pages containing Lincoln's second and subsequent handwritten notes. She said at some point when the book was owned by the Brown brothers it was used as part of a failed exhibit of Lincoln-related materials. This first handwritten page and the facing page of clippings were exposed to light for a considerable period of time. This exposure caused oxidation by which cellulose in the paper broke down and the pages yellowed as they aged.

A one-sentence note in a plastic sleeve is also found in the Huntington's clamshell box containing the notebook. Signed by J. McCan Davis, the *Facsimile's* editor, it states: "Lincoln's part of the book ends here. Pages which follow were prepared subsequently by Mr. Brown." Perhaps it served as a bookmark.

Also in the same clamshell box was a clipping from the original 1914 Lambert auction notice. It described the notebook in detail and states the auction house's conclusion: "nothing more interesting than this little book could be secured by the collector of historical relics." Both this clipping and Davis's 'bookmark' are found below and in the following page.

(An online version of the auction results at https://archive.org/details/libraryoflatemaj00metr/page/68/mode/1up?view=theater shows Smith's initials and the price he paid – $2,250 – clearly visible.)

Seeing this singular book in person is, itself, a Lincoln historian's 'bucket list' experience: coming face-to-face (or, more appropriately,) fingertip-to-fingertip with 164-years of American history. Plus knowing previous Lincoln scholars have trod the same path; examining this simple but extraordinary ephemera which Lincoln himself held and in which he wrote.

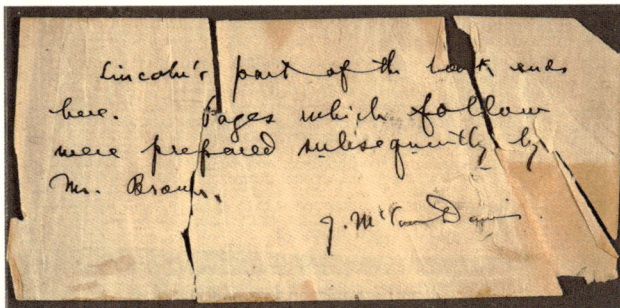

Davis 'bookmark'

LINCOLN'S SCRAPBOOK, MADE FOR CAPTAIN JAMES N. BROWN, AND USED BY HIM IN THE CAMPAIGN OF 1858.

477. LINCOLN (ABRAHAM). Original Note Book in which Lincoln pasted contemporary newspaper accounts of his speeches relating to negro equality; containing manuscript notes by him, and a long autograph letter.

On the inside of the front cover Lincoln has written :—"The following extracts are taken from various speeches of mine delivered at various times and places, and I believe they contain the substance of all I have ever said about 'negro equality.' The first three are from my answer to Judge Douglas, Oct. 16, 1854—at Peoria."

The three newspaper clippings of the speeches follow, pasted down and numbered : On the next page Lincoln has written :— "The fourth extract is from a speech delivered June 26, 1857, at Springfield." The printed speech follows. On the next page is a MSS. note :—"The following marked 5 is from my speech at Chicago, July 10, 1858. Because garbled extracts are often taken from this speech, I have given the whole which touches 'negro equality.' " The printed speeech follows. On the next page there is another note which reads :—"The following marked 6, was brought in immediately after reading the first extract in this scrap-book, in the first joint meeting with Judge Douglas, Aug. 21, 1858 at Ottawa." The reverse has a note :—"The following marked 7 is from my speech at the fourth joint meeting, Sept. 18, 1858, at Charleston."

Following these clippings there is a long autograph letter to "Hon. J. N. Brown," dated Springfield, Oct. 18, 1858, beginning : "I do not perceive how I can express myself more plainly than I have done in the foregoing extracts. In four of them I have expressly disclaimed all intention to bring about social and political equality between the white and black races, and, in all the rest, I have done the same thing by clear implication," etc. This letter occupies 8 pages of the book, and is signed. The remainder of the book is made up of clippings and pencil notes by Mr. Brown. 18mo, worn leather, in a new morocco slip-case.

* Captain Brown, who called himself at this time a "Lincoln Republican," was a man of considerable popularity in Sangamon County. Originally a Whig, and from Kentucky, he found it difficult to answer the artful charges of Douglas and his followers that Lincoln's aim was to put the negroes on a par with the white voters. He wrote to Lincoln that he felt sure these charges were false, but that he had trouble to formulate a convincing denial. In reply Lincoln made up this book to define his position clearly, and Captain Brown carried it with him through the remainder of the campaign, reading from it frequently in public as "Lincoln's own words on the question." Nothing more interesting than this little book could be secured by the collector of historical relics.

Lambert auction sale notice

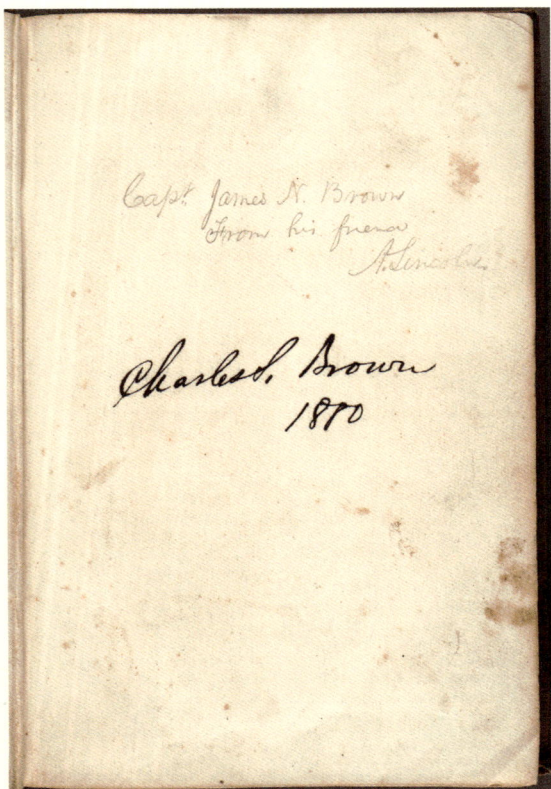

Capt James N. Brown
from his friend
A Lincoln

Charles S. Brown
1870

Lincoln gave Brown a signed first edition of the Follett, Foster and Company 1860 *Political Debates between Hon. Abraham Lincoln and Hon. Stephen A. Douglas"*. Only 42 volumes of the approximately 30,000 – 50,000 copies printed are known to have been autographed by Lincoln. Scan courtesy Huntington Library.]

Appendix D

*Handwritten Notes and Transcripts by
Ida M. Tarbell, William H. Lambert,
and George D. Smith*

Here, in chronological order, are the handwritten notes and transcripts by Ida M. Tarbell, William H. Lambert, and George D. Smith from the "Galena" copy of the 1901 *Facsimile.*

Additionally, appended is the dust jacket cover of Tarbell's 1924 book *In The Footsteps of the Lincolns* and its relevant pages 360-361 which directly led to the publication of *by Abraham Lincoln: His 1858 Time Capsule.*

Ida M. Tarbell

My Dear Mr Miller,

you have asked
me to give you
some information
about the Lincoln-Book.
There is little to
give which is not
to be found in
Mr Davis Introduc-
tory Note. I first
heard of its exis-
tence about three

three years ago when
in Springfield working
after material for
my Latin Life of
Stevens, and asked
Mr Davis who was
assisting me to se-
cure permission
from the owners
to publish the
letter and the
account of the
making of the

book in my desk. They
hesitated so long
however, that I had
to give up publishing
it in the Life.

After long negotia-
tions Mr Davis
secured for him
the right to re-
produce the book
in fac-simile and
a few months
later it was
sold to my

friend Mr Lambert
of Philadelphia.
It is now in his
collection and I
am sure he has
nothing among
his many fine
pieces which he
prizes more.

I believe our
first edition is
1500. and that
the second while

will soon come will
be about 1000 copies

You asked about
the price paid for
the original by
the bookseller with
whom Mr Lambert
had the negotia-
tion. I am not
at liberty to
give it. I am
sorry to say.

Hoping my dear
Mr Miller that
you will enjoy
the fac-simile as
much as I have
the rather slow
task of seeing
it brought to the
public, I am
   Very Sincerely Your
      Ida M. Tarbell
February 23d, 1901

E Abraham Lincoln

My Dear Mr. Miller,

You have asked me to give you some information about the Scrap-book. There is little to give which is not to be found in Mr. Davis introductory note.

I first heard of its existence about some three years ago in Springfield looking after materials for my Later Life of Lincoln and asked of Mr. Davis who was assisting me to secure permission from its owners to publish that letter and the account of the making of the book in my work. They hesitated so long however that I had to give up publishing it in the Life.

After long negotiations Mr. Davis secured for us the right to reproduce the book in fac-simile and a few months later it was sold to my friend Mr. Lambert of Philadelphia. It is now in his collection and I am sure he has nothing among his many fine pieces which he prizes more.

I believe our first edition is 1500 and that the second which will soon come will be about 1000 copies. You asked about the price paid for the original by the bookseller with whom Mr. Lambert had his negotiations. I am not at liberty to give it, I am sorry to say.

Hoping, my dear Mr. Miller that you will enjoy the fac-simile as much as I have the rather slow task of seeing it brought to the public.

I am very sincerely yours,

Ida M. Tarbell
February 23^d, 1901

William H. Lambert

The book of which the important part has been reproduced in facsimile herein is now in my possession. I am indebted to Miss Tarbell for my first knowledge of its existence. Probably I could have obtained the book from the Messrs Brown

three years ago but for
some reason allowed
the opportunity to pass.
Last fall Mr George D
Smith of New York
offered the book and
I accepted it promptly
I value it more highly
because of its unique
personal association
with Abraham Lincoln

I consider the face
Smile an Excellent
reproduction ; the
original

William B Lauton

July 16 1901.

Abraham Lincoln

The book of which the important part has been reproduced in facsimile herein is now in my possession. I am indebted to Miss Tarbell for my first knowledge of its existence.

Probably I could have obtained the book from the Messrs. Brown three years ago but for some reason allowed the opportunity to pass.

Last fall Mr. George D. Smith of New York offered the book and I accepted it promptly. I value it more highly because of its unique personal association with Abraham Lincoln.

I consider the facsimile an excellent reproduction of the original.

William H. Lambert,
July 16, 1901

George D. Smith

I bought the original of this book [from the Brown brothers] and sold it to Major W. H. Lambert of Philadelphia who does not want the price he paid mentioned.

George D. Smith,
Sept. 16, 1901
Lambert Sale – $2250

H|B

In The Footsteps
Of The Lincolns

The story of Abraham Lincoln really be-
gins in 1637. This new story of Lincoln
is here told by his biographer—the narra-
tive of his origin and his family—from the
time the first Lincoln set foot on American soil to Abraham Lincoln himself

Ida M. Tarbell

¶ The rail-splitter, poor white trash stock which
has been popularly accepted as the ancestry of
Abraham Lincoln does not exist. Miss Tarbell
proves it. Not only does she prove it, but she tells
the history of the Lincolns in America since the
seventeenth century in a most fascinating way.

HARPER & BROTHERS, *Publishers*
Established 1817

Dust jacket front cover of Ida M. Tarbell 1924 book
In The Footsteps Of The Lincolns.

IN THE FOOTSTEPS OF THE LINCOLNS

was in a group following Mr. Lincoln up the street in Rushville. The whole population was out, among them many young women prominent in society, some of them, according to Mr. Lowry, "very dark complected." One of these girls, stepping in front of Lincoln, dangled a little negro doll baby in his face. He turned to her quietly and said, "Madam, are you the mother of that?" "It created quite a sensation in that small town," says Mr. Lowry!

The charge that Lincoln believed in "negro equality" finally became so serious an embarrassment to his supporters that one of them, Capt. J. N. Brown, of Berlin, Illinois, asked him for a clear statement which he could use in debates. Lincoln's answer is a fine illustration of the infinite pains the man was willing to take to make a position clear. He bought a little black-covered note book, and in it wrote what we may call the preface—the words reproduced on the next page. Following this he pasted in several newspaper clippings from his speeches, showing exactly his position, and each of these quotations he prefaced by a few written words telling their source. He followed the whole by a letter of 500 words in which he reiterates in brief what he regards as the substance of the extracts that he had given.

The only book by Abraham Lincoln which has ever been published is this little one prepared for Capt. Brown. The late J. McCan Davis of Springfield, Illinois, secured for McClure-Phillips Co., in 1903, the permission to publish it in facsimile, and prepared the introductory note which goes with the book. It is now a rare document, the edition having been exhausted.

At Freeport you will find, not only from your guidebook but from thoughtful inhabitants, if you are lucky enough to meet them, that the feature of the debate there was a question which Lincoln propounded to Douglas, forcing him to make

[360]

Footsteps page 360

149

A VICTORIOUS DEFEAT

an answer showing the inconsistency of his position, his effort
to make the South believe that they could carry their slaves
into the territories, the North to believe that they could keep
them out, in spite of Repeal and Dred Scott decision—a

The following extracts are taken from various speeches of mine delivered at various times and places and I believe they contain the substance of all I have ever said about "Negro equality." The first three are from my answer to Judge Douglas, Oct. 16. 1854 at Peoria—

FACSIMILE OF FOREWORD WRITTEN BY A. LINCOLN IN A CAMPAIGN BOOK
COMPILED BY HIM IN 1858 FOR A FRIEND.

position which Mr. Lincoln aptly characterized later as an
argument that a thing may be lawfully driven away from
where it has a lawful right to be!

And so it goes. At Quincy you will be sure to be told
the story which so delighted its hearers as well as those who
hear it for the first time to-day, of Lincoln's pulling off his

[361]

Footsteps page 361

150

Appendix E

Wendy Allen and Lincoln Into Art

Painter Wendy Allen **(1955-)**, the artist who created the cover and chapter illustrations of *by Abraham Lincoln: His 1858 Time Capsule,* has made her professional life's work portraying the many faces and facets of Abraham Lincoln. Her Lincoln paintings have been exhibited throughout the United States and are collected world-wide.

In her published book *Wendy Allen: Lincoln Into Art, The First Thirty Years (1983 -2013),* Allen explores "the concept of history within the artistic framework of perspective, composition, color and texture."

In 1983, her first Lincoln portrait changed her life. "Finally, my heart and ambition had translated onto canvas. I had gone into Merlin's cave and emerged with the secret of my universe. To me he represented the best of mankind. I had found my passion. And, through my art, the world would take a new look at Abraham Lincoln – the very best that history has to offer."

Allen describes her style as "obsessionist. For me, Lincoln symbolizes wisdom, moral courage, and the promise of freedom. Painting his face over and over again – in different manners and techniques – has become my life's passion. I am an obsessionist. My painting is obsessive because freedom is never finished."

Allen found her inspiration for this book's cover from Harold Holzer's *Lincoln at Cooper Union*. While Holzer described an 1859 moment, it could equally have been October 1858. "Here, his head characteristically resting on his thumb, his index finger curved across his lips and up the side of his nose, his other four fingers tightly clenched . . . [Lincoln] would set his elbow on the table, place his chin in his hand and 'maintain this position as immovable as a statue'. . . lost in thought . . . 'oblivious to all else.'"

The cover art portrays the thoughtful un-bearded Lincoln writing his notes to campaigner James N. Brown. As noted, the portrait's background palette is the brooding, almost ominous antebellum gray clouds that unmistakably hung over the 1858 campaign.

And in his introduction to *Wendy Allen: Lincoln Into Art,* Holzer praises Allen's "nuanced, earnest, subtle, impressionistic, magical interpretations of Lincoln [bringing] moments in time to full life and deeper understanding, while leaving the viewer with unanswered, thought-provoking questions."

Allen's studio/gallery is located in Gettysburg, Pennsylvania on Baltimore Street, the once dusty way on which Lincoln travelled on November 19, 1863.

Wendy Allen

Appendix F

Huntington Library Lincoln "Scrapbook" Provenance

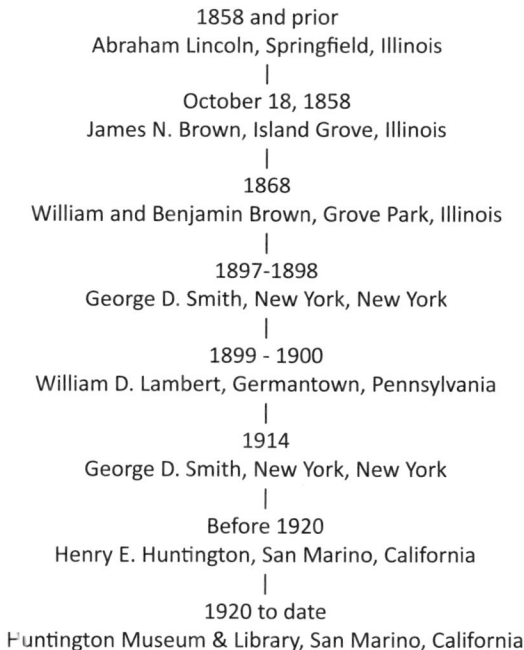

1858 and prior
Abraham Lincoln, Springfield, Illinois
|
October 18, 1858
James N. Brown, Island Grove, Illinois
|
1868
William and Benjamin Brown, Grove Park, Illinois
|
1897-1898
George D. Smith, New York, New York
|
1899 - 1900
William D. Lambert, Germantown, Pennsylvania
|
1914
George D. Smith, New York, New York
|
Before 1920
Henry E. Huntington, San Marino, California
|
1920 to date
Huntington Museum & Library, San Marino, California

The Abraham Lincoln Presidential Library and Museum

Appendix G

Leonard Volk Bust of Lincoln

This 15-inch-tall bust of Abraham Lincoln was gifted by sculptor Leonard Wells Volk to Lincoln after he won the Republican presidential nomination in 1860. It was then given by Lincoln to a friend and neighbor, the Rev. Noyes Miner, when Lincoln moved from Springfield, Illinois to Washington, DC in February 1861. It is now in the permanent collection of the Abraham Lincoln Presidential Library and Museum in Springfield; a gift of Illinois First Lady MK Pritzker, who purchased it for $400,000 in 2022 from Heritage Auctions in Dallas.

Artist Douglas Volk used other copies of this bust in his portraiture of Lincoln.

Sculptor Leonard Wells Volk's bust of Abraham Lincoln.
Photo courtesy Heritage Auctions

Abraham Lincoln's Springfield, Illinois home.

If Lincoln Were Alive Today…

Abraham Lincoln's writings are finite, but his influence ripples through the ages.

This book encapsulates Lincoln's 1858 thinking on a very fraught subject.

Now, imagine a time capsule to be opened in 87 years on Lincoln's 300th birthday: February 12, 2109. As Harold Holzer suggests in his opening essay, 'use these blank pages to record your own thoughts on the divisive issues we confront more than a century-and-a-half after Lincoln engaged Douglas on the subject of race in America.'

Abraham Lincoln

Abraham Lincoln

E Abraham Lincoln

About the Script Vectors and Typeface

The script vector of Lincoln's signature is publicly available from many documents he signed with his full name.

The vector of the word "by" atop all left-hand pages comes from Lincoln's letter to James N. Brown.

The vector of James N. Brown's signature has been taken from a contemporary document he signed.

This book is typeset in Calibri, a sans-serif typeface designed by Luc(as) de Groot in 2002-2004. It was chosen for its 21st century lineage, its readability, and its deliberate contrast to the 19th century typefaces found in other portions of this book. Which typefaces, according to 1901 Publisher McClure Phillips & Co.'s note reproduced in Appendix D, were chosen "for [their] likeness to a kind popular in country newspaper offices at the time Mr. Lincoln compiled the book."

About the Graphic Designer

Diane K. Nichols has worked as a graphic designer for more than 30 years. She is a sculptor and passionate nature lover. She currently lives in central Pennsylvania at the foothills of the Tuscarora Mountains.

Abraham Lincoln

About the Editor

Ross E. Heller

In yet another of this book's coincidences, the lives of Ida M. Tarbell and that of **Ross E. Heller (1943 –)** actually intersected during the years 1943 – 1944. In some mystic way, perhaps, he and she thus share the Lincoln time capsule's continuity from the 19th into the 21st century.

In his career Mr. Heller, holder of a B.A. in History from Clark University and an M.A. in Journalism from the University of Oregon, has been a journalist, U.S. Senate press secretary, lobbyist, association executive, entrepreneur, newspaper publisher and now, editor/author. Researching this book, he is also discoverer of new facts of America's most-storied life; a life about which no one could imagine anything new could *ever* be found.

Ida Tarbell's 1924 *In the Footsteps of the Lincolns* led to his search for the full story of 1901's *Abraham Lincoln: His Book.* These discoveries have now provided a better understanding that *that* book is, truly, Lincoln's 1858 time capsule gift to the nation whose promise he so cherished.

That the "Galena" copy of the *Facsimile* will be available to all, it has been donated to the Abraham Lincoln Presidential Library and Museum in Springfield, Illinois. And to further enhance continuing Lincoln scholarship, a portion of this book's proceeds will be donated to the Lincoln Forum and the Lincoln Presidential Foundation.

Mr. Heller lives in Chevy Chase, Maryland.

Abraham Lincoln

Acknowledgements

by Abraham Lincoln was provided imprimatur by the Special Introduction from the inestimable Harold Holzer. He is author, among other Lincoln volumes, of *Lincoln at Cooper Union*, *Lincoln President-Elect* and *Lincoln and the Power of the Press*, as well as Chairman of The Lincoln Forum. Thank you, Harold, for your friendship and, of course, your generous and warm introductory essay.

And since no Abraham Lincoln story can be without images of the 16th President, this book has three paintings and one sculptural bust.

Renowned Lincoln portrait artist Wendy Allen of Gettysburg, Pennsylvania provided the two splendid pieces of original art that grace the dust jacket, cover, and chapter title pages. They perfectly capture the contemplative, still un-bearded, Lincoln at a break from 1858 campaigning writing notes for James Brown's use.

Regarding Douglas Volk's 1928 "La Jolla Lincoln," Art Conservator Joy Hallman of Montgomery Village, Maryland brought out highlights long obscured by generations of politicians' cigar smoke and brandy fumes deposited at original owner James S. Copley's La Jolla, California library.

Todd McElwee, Hagerstown, Maryland, *USAE* Associate Publisher, provided valuable research. Cheryl A. Adamscheck of Seaside, Oregon gave always gentle, but valuable criticism. Jane Hartqu st, of Chevy Chase, Maryland did genealogical research. Stacie Nerf and Patrick Pickens of Delta Air Lines, Atlanta, Georgia suggested valuable additions as did first cousins Joyce Prescott and Marilyn Waff both of Eugene, Oregon. Mary Power, of Alexandria, Virginia, a wise member of my extended association community family, offered the thought-provoking "time capsule" concept and challenge.

E Abraham Lincoln

A very special 'thank you' to William L. Butts of Galena, Illinois. While serendipity brought us together, Bill's generosity allowed the "Galena" edition of the *Facsimile* to come to the Abraham Lincoln Presidential Library and Museum.

Glenna Schroeder-Lein of Springfield, Illinois, accurately transcribed the difficult-to-read 19th-century script of James N. Brown as well as the 20th-century handwriting of Ida M. Tarbell, William H. Lambert and George D. Smith. And thank you, also, Lincoln historian James Cornelius. Lastly, Lincoln author and historian Allen Ottens of Rockford, Illinois provided valuable criticism.

This book's superb graphics and design are thanks to Diane K. Nichols of Mercersburg, Pennsylvania, creative director *USAE* weekly newspaper. Sandy Smith of Mt. Juliet, Tennessee is the talented creator of the book's website *byabrahamlincolnbook. com*.

For on-target marketing advice and detailed editorial sugges-tions, thank you, Vancouver, British Columbia travel author Rick Antonson. Rick Sauers, former President of the Sauers Group, Stone Mountain, Georgia, provided extraordinary production counsel.

Lastly, thank you sons James A. Heller, Christopher E. Heller and Patrick D. Heller for your continuing support.

Any errors are my responsibility.

Ross E. Heller
Chevy Chase, Maryland
September 2022